Praise for Joy

# Put a Cherry on Top:
# Generosity in Life & Leadership

*"Put a Cherry on Top* is a delightful and insightful gem –
a must-read for all who aspire to be better leaders
and human beings."

— SUSAN PACKARD, Co-Founder, HGTV; Author, *New
Rules of the Game; Fully Human*

"Read this book. Joyce Russell's fresh, funny, and wise
insights about life and work will inspire and energize you."

— BILLIE JEAN KING, Founder, Billie Jean King
Leadership Initiative

"A must-read to inject optimism and motivation into your
regular routine. This will mean the world to your team.
Joyce's passion is contagious!"

— KATE GUTMANN, Chief Sales and Solutions
Officer, UPS

"Joyce Russell is a brilliant leader who knows that people are
motivated by personal attention and real connection. This is
what drives all of us to achieve our highest potential."

— LAURIE ANN GOLDMAN, Board Director and
Former CEO, Spanx and Avon

"Joyce Russell's life and leadership lessons about integrity and sharing the best of ourselves are at the heart of winning in life and leaving a legacy. The cherry on top of this book is Joyce herself: she is relatable, authentic, and committed to growing the next generation of women leaders."

— MINDY MEADS, Chairman of Zenith WPO and Former CEO of Lands' End, CEO of Victoria's Secret Direct, and CO-CEO of Aeropostale

"Joyce's values, generosity, and enthusiasm for life as a business leader and a human being shine through each page of her book. She teaches us that we can all choose to 'put a cherry on top' to enrich each life we touch. This must-read will help you achieve your goals and get the most out of each day."

— GAY GADDIS, Founder, T3; CEO, Gay Gaddis, LLC; Author, *Cowgirl Power: How to Kick Ass in Business and Life*

"Joyce Russell candidly shares her experiences that helped her achieve great career success and a rich, rewarding personal life. Anyone who aspires to a life of professional and personal success, filled with joy and meaningful relationships, will appreciate Joyce's wisdom."

— LINDA L. ADDISON, Independent Director and Immediate Past Managing Partner, Norton Rose Fulbright US LLP

"Joyce Russell's leadership journey took her to the top of one of the largest employers on the planet. In this book, she shares the strategies that got her there. Joyce becomes our professional mentor and personal friend as she shares her optimism and philosophy on life, work, and family in this enlightening book."

— ROBIN MEE, President, Mee Derby

"Get ready to feel all the feels as Joyce Russell guides you along a delightful and heartwarming personal journey. You will learn how to become a better leader from one of the best. This highly relatable, honest, and witty compilation of anecdotes is a must-read for anyone looking to make a real and lasting impact on people."

— LESLIE VICKREY, CEO and Founder, ClearEdge Marketing

"Joyce Russell delivers in 'Cherry on Top' – a must-read for up and coming leaders. Joyce teaches us that leadership is personal, relationships matter, and going above and beyond IS EVERYTHING! Having worked with Joyce for over 20 years I can attest she is the real deal – earnest, authentic, and a generous spirit."

— SANDI HOKANSSON, Executive Coach and CEO, SOUNDLEADERSHIP Inc.

"This book should be required reading for today's young people as they search for success. It is an inspiration for living your life to the fullest, personally and professionally. Joyce genuinely embodies the message of excellence, effort, and service each day. She knows how these attitudes and actions can change lives, overcome challenges, and grow successful, world-class businesses."

— KENNETH BUCKLEY, Assistant Dean of Career Management, Baylor University

"Joyce Russell is the real deal. Her story will inspire you to live beyond everyone's wildest expectations — including your own."

— JOHN FOLEY, Former Lead Solo Pilot, Blue Angels; Founder and CEO, CenterPoint Companies

# Put a Cherry on Top

## on Top

### GENEROSITY IN
### LIFE & LEADERSHIP

## Joyce Russell
with Sarah Davis

Joyce Russell
Put a Cherry on Top: Generosity in Life & Leadership

ISBN 978-0-578-64928-3

Edited by Adrienne Hand
Copyedit by Sheila Gibbons Hiebert
Graphic Design by Alexis Chng-Castor

Contact: info@acherryontopbook.com

Publisher's Cataloging-in-Publication Data

Names: Russell, Joyce E. A., author. | Davis, Sarah P., author.
Title: Put a cherry on top: generosity in life and leadership /
Joyce Russell; with Sarah Davis.
Description: Includes bibliographical references. |
Vero Beach, FL: Collier Publishing, 2020.
Identifiers: ISBN 978-0-578-64928-3
Subjects: LCSH Leadership. | Leadership--Anecdotes. |
Management. | Success in business. | Generosity. |
Self-management (Psychology) | Conduct of life. | BISAC
BUSINESS & ECONOMICS / Leadership
Classification: LCC HD57.7 .R864 2019 | DDC 650.1--dc23

## TO MY PARENTS

For the gift of a happy childhood and for teaching my
sisters and me about kindness and generosity

## TO DAVID

For allowing me to be a butterfly and for being the
best dad to Bryson and Coleman

## TO THE TALENTED & PASSIONATE
## PEOPLE OF ADECCO

Whom I am proud to call colleagues and friends

# Note from Author

For many years, I talked about writing a book. Like the "Five Frogs on a Log", I had decided to write a book, but somehow never actually got around to doing it. Without the help and encouragement from two very special people, I would still be doing a lot of "talking," and not a lot of "doing" - actually writing a book.

From this experience, I learned that writing a book is a lot harder than I thought. Although I had many stories, ideas, and experiences to share, I didn't really know how to tell my story in a meaningful way. I needed help, and I was lucky to have my "senior most trusted advisor" of many years, Sarah Davis, help me bring the book to life. Sarah and I had a "book file" where we saved stories, notes, and ideas that we would include in a book, one day. Thanks to Sarah and her high sense of urgency and organizational skills, we got started by writing the first chapter. From there, we "jumped off the log," and committed to finishing the book.

Relationships matter, and my good friend Robin Mee introduced me to Adrienne Hand, a book editor based in Bethesda, Maryland. I had considered other editors, but getting a personal reference from a friend I trusted, was huge. As an editor, Adrienne was my cheerleader, grammar expert, and trail guide; she kept me on task and managed the project from concept to delivery. As I say, "There are very few special people," and I would most certainly put Adrienne in that category. Adrienne's extra touches and attention to detail were the cherry on top of the entire experience, and I am exceptionally grateful for her editing expertise and friendship.

Finally, thank you to Alexis Chng-Castor for her design skills and positive attitude, and for helping me to make this a beautiful book.

– Joyce

# CONTENTS

# Introduction: The Beginning

I was born on Mother's Day in Pompano Beach, Florida. My great-great-grandfather was born in Florida in 1845, so I am a fifth-generation Floridian. According to family history, at least three of my great-great-grandfathers were farmers, and my father Wayne was a tomato farmer and citrus grower. My mother Ruth stayed at home most of my life, and later was a teacher who worked with students to help them learn, study, and prepare to pass the Florida literacy exam.

My mother has a giving heart. I can remember many occasions when she took in people who were "down on their luck," allowing them to stay in our comfortable guest house until their situation improved. My father has always been kind, as well. Even today, when we are out to dinner at a restaurant, he will make a point to genuinely compliment the waitress and say something nice: "Delores, you have the prettiest brown eyes." Delores' face lights up, and I know that Dad has just made her day. Being nice doesn't cost anything, and the returns are immeasurable. I learned from my parents the sincere desire to be kind and help others. They showed me that generosity and helpfulness are simply a way of life.

My sisters Karyn, Kristi and I were very fortunate to have been raised by such loving and wonderful parents who set an example for us and have been role models for us throughout our lives. When we were little girls, we followed Mom and Dad around like three little ducklings. Along the way, we were imprinted with life lessons, big and small, that would shape us into the people we are today. "Thankful" feels inadequate to express the gratitude I have for my parents' giving us a happy childhood and a firm foundation on which to grow and develop. We were blessed beyond measure.

I remember many adventures we had growing up. Summer in Florida is not growing season and school is out until mid-August. For the Collier family, summer was family travel time. My parents would pack up the red Chrysler Newport with a white vinyl roof and take me and Karyn and Kristi on road trips across America.

Our personalities were formed at an early age. We each had a nickname: Karyn, the oldest, was Montanya. I am the middle child, nicknamed Bombalita by my father because I was spunky and full of energy. And Kristi, the youngest, was Baby Tuta. Baby Tuta always sat up front between Mom and Dad, while Karyn and I were assigned to the back seat where we argued and aggravated each other. My sweet mother attempted to keep the peace between us by monitoring our behavior from her passenger-side vanity mirror. Every trip was a new adventure in learning.

We visited 49 states, crisscrossing America from Portland, Maine, to Portland, Oregon, and everywhere in between. We visited the Grand Canyon, the museums of Washington, DC, the Golden Gate Bridge, and the Native American reservations outside of Santa Fe, where we purchased turquoise jewelry.

Most nights, we stayed at the Holiday Inn, where "Kids Stay and Eat Free." What I remember most about these trips is that my mother and father always made an effort to make our experiences just a little bit better by doing something unexpected and thoughtful. It might be a surprise dinner at

Kristi, Karyn, and me (Baby Tuta, Montanya, and Bombalita)

the Rainbow Room in New York City, or ice skating at the Broadmoor Hotel in Colorado Springs, Colorado. Whatever it was, it was always a surprise that created wonderful memories of our trip.

This delightful surprise is what I call "putting a cherry on top." It's about thoughtfulness: the extra effort and attention to detail that makes everything just a little bit better. A cherry on top expresses love and appreciation for others. Putting a cherry on top in the staffing industry means going above and beyond what is expected and creating truly memorable experiences that build strong relationships and client loyalty. A cherry on top is what the French call "la cerise sur le gâteau" – the icing on the cake, or the final touch that makes something perfect.

My love of business and sales started when I was in middle school. In the tomato business in Florida, the season ends in May. When I was 14, and we were all gathered around the dining room table, my father would sometimes ask, "Who wants the field before Heinz and Hunts make ketchup?" My hand was the first to shoot straight up in the air to claim the field. What Dad was asking me, Karyn, and Kristi was: Did one of us want to scramble out to our farm field to scoop up the remaining tomatoes on the ground before they were sold off for ketchup? I loved winning the field because that meant I could set up my card table and tackle box (my cash register) and sell the tomatoes at the Pompano Beach city farmer's market.

I wore blue jeans, tennis shoes, and my hair was pulled back in a ponytail with a hot pink ribbon. One of the best lessons I learned about business was from behind that card table. I had 24 red buckets set up, each containing tomatoes that I had picked in the same field. Here's what would happen: One woman would begin selecting tomatoes out of one of the buckets. Before I knew it, there were two to three other people around the exact same bucket picking tomatoes. What I noticed was that although there were 23 other buckets, all identical, they somehow thought the best tomatoes were in that one bucket.

When I started working in the staffing industry in 1987 at Adia, a Swiss-based staffing company founded in 1957, we used the tomato bucket lesson to grow our business. At that time, there were two regional banks that were the best places to work in Charlotte, and still are. We knew that if we could win these accounts, we would own the market because these top two companies were where people wanted to work. Working with the banks gave Adia cachet as the top staffing company to work with for landing temporary and permanent jobs with the most prestigious companies in town. We had the best employers in our "bucket," and that helped us grow our reputation and our revenue.

Another business lesson I learned when I was young was in the strawberry fields. My father offered a "You Pick" for customers wanting strawberries and tomatoes. I noticed that women would pull up in their Cadillacs fresh from the beauty parlor with their hair perfect and set for the week. I knew that these women did not want to go out in the fields in their nice shoes and make-up to pick strawberries in the dirt and heat of south Florida humidity. Right then, I saw an opportunity, and I hustled for it.

Every morning, I arrived early and headed straight out to the fields by myself to pick strawberries. Being the first one out in the field for the day meant that I had "first dibs" on the best berries. By the time the ladies arrived, I had already picked and arranged the strawberries in plastic buckets and placed them at the stand. There was no need for the ladies to get out of their car, mess up their hair, or get sweaty. Dad paid me $1.25 for every basket that was sold, and I was thrilled.

When I was in college, I worked at Mary Webb's, a boutique bridal shop. This was a dream job. It was pure joy to help women find their perfect wedding gown. It was there that I learned about incentive selling. I was given a bonus for each wedding gown I sold.

I sold so many dresses that one day, Mary Webb's son Grey (who worked in the family business) said to me, "Joyce, you have to stop selling wedding dresses." When I asked, "Why?" Grey said, "You are selling too many, and I can't afford to pay you." That didn't make any sense to me, because I couldn't understand how selling more wedding dresses could be a bad thing. Selling was fun for me, and making more money for every dress I sold was the cherry on top.

These early selling experiences were formative to my work ethic and life purpose. When I was 27 years old, I brought those lessons and my excitement about selling into the staffing industry – which is a perfect fit for me. By nature, I am an extrovert who strives to create strong relationships and memorable experiences. I am optimistic and a very positive person, and I love to sell! One of my friends refers to me as the "quintessential people person in the people business."

I have been with Adecco Staffing US for 32 years, rising from branch manager to president. I love what I do and I feel blessed to have had so many Cherry on Top opportunities and moments in my career. I really enjoy describing what I do. Often, this opportunity comes up on an airplane flight.

When Adecco acquired Olsten Corporation in 2000, our corporate headquarters moved from Redwood City, California, to Melville, New York on Long Island. Almost every week, I would hop on the Monday morning Charlotte - LaGuardia flight. The plane was full of bankers from Charlotte traveling to the city for meetings. Invariably, shortly after takeoff, one of these bankers would lean over and ask me, "So, what do you do?" (the standard conversation ice breaker on a business flight). I would smile, pause, and in a low whisper respond, "I'm a matchmaker." After waiting for the shocked (and maybe embarrassed) expression, I would continue, "I connect the best talent with the best companies." From there, the conversation naturally flowed into a dialogue about Adecco and my role.

In January of 2019, I became president of The Adecco Group US Foundation, which is dedicated to making the world of work a fairer, more accessible, and better place. Our vision is of a world where all people are enabled to reach their full potential.

This is the perfect culmination of my life and my career. I have tried to live my life in such a way as to bring joy, happiness, and a special surprise to others at every opportunity. Whenever I can, whether at work or at home, I put a cherry on top. It is a big part of who I am.

I have come to realize that the Cherry on Top Lessons I learned in the tomato and strawberry fields, in the backseat of our Chrysler on family trips, and in the bridal shop have stayed with me during my adult life. They have helped to make me a better wife, mother, friend, colleague, and leader.

While this book draws much from my wonderful experiences during my 30+ years with Adecco, the lessons, personal views, and opinions in this book are my own.

# Cherry on Top #1: People are Your DNA

In 1986, I was living in Pompano Beach and working at Great American Farms, a produce brokerage company. One evening, my parents hosted a Young Life fundraiser at their farm, and the emcee of the evening was Jim Nelson. Jim's roommate was David Russell. Jim introduced us, and David and I went on one date. My first impression of David was that he had a great job, was smart, handsome, and a strong Christian – all qualities that were important to me.

A year later, on June 22, we had our second date in Charlotte, and the magic happened. I was on my way to Newton Grove, North Carolina, to purchase produce to sell to the chain grocery stores. David was working for SmithKline Beecham. He had recently been promoted to district manager and had relocated from South Florida to Charlotte. Four months later, on October 24, 1987, we were married in Pompano Beach in the Methodist church on Third Street I attended growing up. As I tell my friends, I married in the infatuation stage, and I highly recommend staying there. To quote H. Jackson Brown, Jr., author of *Life's Little Instruction Book*, "Marry the right person. This one decision will determine 90% of your happiness or misery."

I am lucky David chose me. He has always supported me in my career, and that has allowed me to fly, literally and figuratively. I knew that David had everything covered at home. Our sons Bryson and Coleman had a wonderful, loving, and devoted dad taking care of them while I was traveling on business all over the United States and the world.

The week after a special honeymoon at the lovely

Caneel Bay Resort on St. John, US Virgin Islands, I started a new job as branch manager at Adia in Charlotte. Adia merged with Ecco (a French staffing company) in 1996 to become Adecco – the largest workforce solutions company in the world, operating in more than 60 countries. The Adecco Group is a Fortune Global 500 company, and one of the largest employers in the world.

Staffing is a highly competitive industry with many local, regional, and national companies competing to earn the right to place high-quality talent with premier employers. As an Adia branch manager in 1987, my job was to grow the company's market share in Charlotte by placing more temporary associates at more client companies every week.

My job was thrilling to me. I was running a two-million-dollar business with the help of a large corporation. I was responsible for the staff, clients, and associates, and I managed my own profit and loss statement ("P&L"). I was successful in getting new orders from managers and those in charge of making the hiring decisions about temps at their companies.

In staffing, revenue is generated by placing a temporary associate on an assignment. At the end of the week, the associate submits their hours worked for the week via a timecard. The associate receives a paycheck, and the client is invoiced. The more people you have working on assignment, the more sales are being generated for the office.

I understood the industry very well, and I knew what I needed to do as a manager in order to be successful. I knew that to compete and win in this industry, I needed the very best people on my team. My team of recruiters would need to work hard to fill every order with the very best candidates to send to our new accounts. We needed to provide clients and associates with a high level of service. So I hired people with a high sense of urgency, a strong work ethic, and the ability to create relationships with our dual clientele: the key contacts at our client companies and our temporary associates who worked on assignments.

I love people with a high sense of urgency because they do things now rather than later; they act quickly, they accomplish tasks, and they solve problems. People who lack a sense of urgency procrastinate, wait, and most often explain their lack of action and effort with "I was gonna," meaning they were going to act sometime in the future, but not now. Let me tell you something: when someone in our house hasn't taken the trash out four hours after being asked, my response to "I was gonna," is "I didda."

It was at Adia that I discovered the value of a high-performing team of doers. I knew that I could work hard and that I would be successful selling new accounts and getting new orders. That was the easy part for me. But to grow our business and exceed our goals, my team needed to match my level of excitement, enthusiasm, and sense of urgency. They needed to fill those orders with the very best candidates and to get more associates working – week after week.

It was during my two years as branch manager that I learned about employee motivation, trust, recognition, and holding people accountable. Although we had a robust training program, much of what I learned was "on-the-job training." I learned something new every single day about how to be a "manager." I must have done something right, because in 1988, I was honored with Adia's Rookie of the Year award.

In January 1989, Adia opened a second office in Charlotte, and I was promoted to area manager. Four months later, I was promoted to area vice president of the Southeast Area. I now had the responsibility of six offices: two in Charlotte, two in Birmingham, one in Louisville, and one in Richmond. I was excited about the promotion and the challenge. Now I had more responsibility, more people who reported to me, and of course, a larger budget and high expectations from Adia's management team.

My new direct report team included six branch managers. Everyone had to perform in order for us to make our numbers. There was a saying during that time, "You're only as good as your last operating statement." I felt the pressure to perform, and I was highly motivated to be successful. I came to understand how I would achieve stellar results – by hiring, developing, and retaining talent. These were the most important things I did as area vice president.

I also learned how to be a better manager, someone that others would want to work for and follow. I learned about creating experiences for colleagues, and my focus was always putting a cherry on top – creating a thrilling, unexpected, and memorable experience.

In May 1990, I wanted to bring my team together for a meeting. It's easy to plan a team meeting in a building conference room or a hotel meeting room in any city. I wanted to do something more for my team, to bring us all together and to share a special experience. So, instead of meeting in Charlotte, or Richmond, or Louisville or Birmingham in a sterile meeting room with no windows and catered hotel food, I decided to hold our meeting in Hilton Head, South Carolina.

Of course, everyone was very excited when they heard this news – Hilton Head is beautiful, and the weather in May is perfect. But the cherry on top that made the experience extra special was that I invited spouses and children to join us for the weekend. Listen, one of the best things you can do for your colleagues is to do something nice for their children or family. Including families in our meeting created a tremendous bonding and relationship-building experience. We didn't just have a team meeting in Hilton Head. That in and of itself was a treat. The cherry on top for my colleagues was looking around and seeing family members smiling and happy on the beach together for the weekend.

Both inside and outside of the office, my focus was always on growing and developing my team. I was working with them side by side, leading by example, making work fun, recognizing performance, and always giving constructive feedback. In 1989, we received the Area of the Year award.

In every subsequent role, I believed it was my job to identify and grow the future leaders of our company. That's where I put my energy and my focus: on talent – my favorite thing. Talent is the most important, invigorating, and tenuous part of every company's DNA. I believe that talent is absolutely the most essential piece of every high-performing organization. Because our talent, our DNA, determines who we are. It's what makes us special, and it is what differentiates us. Our talent defines everything about us – our culture, our energy, our competitive advantage, and ultimately our position in the marketplace.

## Cherry on Top #2:
## Talent is the Biggest Rock in the Jar

One of my favorite metaphors is expressed in the story, "The Big Rocks in the Jar." I love it because it is easy to explain and it provides a strong visual image about accomplishing the important things and managing the minuscule.

Talent is the most important, invigorating and tenuous part of every company's DNA.

Imagine for a moment a glass jar that is five inches in circumference and 10 inches high. Next to the jar, you have five big rocks, about the size of your fist. And next to the rocks, you have four cups of beach sand. Your goal is to fill up the jar with the rocks and the sand.

At face value, that sounds pretty simple. But think about what happens if you first fill up the jar with the sand, and then place the rocks in the jar, on top. The rocks don't fit, because most of the space in the jar is already taken up with sand. What happens if you put the big rocks in first? You can pour the sand in after, and it cascades and fits easily between the rocks. The lesson of the story is that if we accomplish our most important priorities first, "the big rocks," we can then accomplish the small things more easily. If we spend all of our time at work focused on the small inconsequential tasks, "the sand," we will never find time to work on what's really important, "the big rocks." It's very easy to get caught in the quicksand and see entire days and weeks melt away without tackling the major items that need to be completed on your "to do" list. There are distractions every day and everywhere you look. It takes discipline and a conscious effort, but you have to use your time working on the "big rocks" – the priorities that have the largest impact and move your business forward.

I believe that talent is the biggest rock in the jar. People are everything. As a leader, that's where I spend my time and put my focus. Because people – our talent – are the single most important contributors to our success, I view talent management as my most important job as a leader. Recruiting, hiring, training, developing, and retaining the next generation of leaders is always my number one priority. With every hire I make, I want to top-grade the organization.

Talent is the new currency. The first time I attended the World Economic Forum in Davos in 2013, there were at least 14 sessions on the subject of talent. If hiring great talent for your team is the greatest contributor to your success, then you must make it a priority, a "big rock." Put first things first. The first big rock is recruiting and hiring outstanding talent for your team.

Before you start recruiting externally, reach out to your own network for referrals, because good people know other good people. Tell them about the position and the type of person you are looking for, and include an overview of

**Ignore the noise. Conquer the critical. Manage the minutiae.**
— Rory Vaden

the role and the hard and soft skills that an ideal candidate would possess. Then ask the question, "Who do you know?" Leverage your relationships to find star candidates. This is a great way to find passive candidates who aren't actively looking for a new opportunity, but who might be a perfect fit for the role and your company. To have someone you know and trust vouch for someone – to give a candidate their personal endorsement – is huge. Hiring through referrals saves time and money, and best of all, you know you are starting with high-quality candidates.

As I mentioned earlier, in April 1989 I was promoted from area manager, when I had responsibility for two offices in Charlotte, to area vice president, a role that included more offices and geography. I now had P&L responsibility for six offices, and I moved from managing my branch and one other branch to six direct reports. Four months later, in August 1989, Stephen Covey's book, *The 7 Habits of Highly Effective People*, was published. On the bookshelf in my office, I have over 200 books, but it is Covey's "7 Habits" that truly resonated with me as a new leader and still do now, 30 years later.

Covey's third habit is "Put First Things First." He tells us that leaders can distinguish among these four quadrants: Urgent – Not Urgent – Important – Not Important. Leaders spend their time in the Urgent and Important quadrants, while managers stay busy working in the Not Important and Not Urgent quadrants.

**Urgent**
- Preparing a major sales presentation
- Writing annual performance reviews
- Launching a new product
- Creating and executing a social media plan
- Finalizing the annual budget
- Following up on action items from a customer meeting

**"Put first things first"**
*The 7 Habits of Highly Effective People*
— Steven Covey

**Not Urgent**
- Cleaning up computer files
- Organizing your desk
- Answering emails
- Talking on the phone catching up with co-workers
- Preparing an expense report
- Spending time on non-critical tasks that are not time-sensitive

One of the best leaders I have ever worked for was Ray Roe, and it always makes me smile when I think of Ray walking around the second floor of our corporate headquarters, singing the Joni Mitchell tune, "Big Yellow Taxi." While I was writing this book, on August 20, 2019, my friend and mentor left us to pave paradise. Ray was a kid from the Bronx, and his father made a living by fixing gumball machines. Ray was not expected to go to college, nor could his parents afford to pay for a college education. In high school, Ray could run fast, and he ended up earning a track scholarship to the U.S. Military Academy at West Point.

As Ray told the story, "I didn't finish at the top of my class, and I wasn't at the very bottom of my class; I enjoyed my experience at West Point and being in the Army." Ray was selected for promotion to Brigadier General in December 1989, 22 years after graduating from West Point. He was the second in his class to be selected for promotion to general officer. Ray was 44 years old and one of the youngest generals in the Army at that time.

After Ray retired from the Army, he moved to the private sector, and from 2004 to 2007, he served as the CEO of the Adecco Group North America. Although running a large staffing company is much different from commanding a tank battalion, Ray was a fantastic leader and mentor. I appreciated the fact that he always said exactly what was on his mind. One of the things Ray told me that I've never forgotten is, "Joyce, we don't have room at our company for jerks."

*The Merriam-Webster Dictionary* defines a *jerk* as:
a. an annoyingly stupid or foolish person
b: an unlikeable person, *especially*: one who is cruel, rude, or small-minded

Ray was right. Jerks have low emotional intelligence ("EQ")

and can wreak havoc on a team and your culture. This is another reason why personal referrals are so valuable when hiring new colleagues for your team/company.

Every hire you make has an impact on the organization, either positive or negative. With each new hire, you are leaving your handprint on the organization. You will be remembered by the people you hired, developed, and mentored; that's how you leave a legacy. At Adecco, I thought of hiring as growing my "family tree."

Here's how my family tree grew: I was fortunate enough to hire a senior leader of sales and member of my team, "Katie." In 2016, Katie and her team were asked to deliver $90 million in new revenue, and they brought $136 million in net new revenue. Katie hired "John," who won a huge multi-million-dollar national account for us. The tree grew some more when John referred "Eric." Each year, the tree has expanded and flourished with new growth. Eric referred "Susan," who referred a future Rookie of the Year Branch Manager, "Matthew."

"The true meaning of life is to plant trees, under whose shade you do not expect to sit."
— Nelson Henderson

I believe that success in business can be attributed to three words: *People. People. People.* That's why I recommend that you hire slow and fire fast. Recruiting and selecting talent is the most important job for a leader, so it's important that you take your time and get it right. Like any important relationship, it takes time to get to know someone, and that can't be done carelessly or without due diligence. Rushing to make an offer to a new hire is like getting engaged after the first date; neither usually works out well for anyone.

I'm a huge advocate of "behavioral interviewing." Behavioral interviewing is based on the idea that past performance predicts future performance. By asking candidates specific questions about what they did in the past, we gain insight into how they will perform/respond in the future. In the staffing business, it's common for recruiters and managers to be interrupted, to have to "change horses in midstream," and deal with unexpected events. One of my favorite interview questions is, "Tell me about a time when you were inconvenienced and had to change your plans to accommodate the wishes, wants, and needs of someone else."

Another question I frequently ask is, "Tell me a success story in your life before the age of 18." After asking this question, I stop talking and wait for the response. Silence. Sometimes the silence can be uncomfortable, but it's important to be quiet and resist the urge to jump in and "rescue" the candidate by suggesting possible answers or by asking follow-up questions. The best answers will sound something like this: "When I was 13, my Girl Scout cookie goal was 150 boxes. I created a special flyer that I emailed to everyone I knew, asking them to buy two boxes. I also worked on Saturdays and Sundays at my brother's hockey games, went door to door in my neighborhood, and set up a table in my mother's office building downtown during winter break. I sold 283 boxes." What that story tells me is that the candidate started a track record of success and a work ethic at an early age. The candidate is goal-oriented and results-driven.

By asking the right questions and listening, you can learn a lot about a candidate: IQ and EQ (social acumen), emotional stability, verbal skills, energy level, sense of urgency, sense of humor, warmth and likeability, and maybe even what's going on in their personal lives. I have been using behavioral interviewing for most of my career, and there is one interview that I will never forget.

I met the candidate at the Charlotte airport to interview him for a management-level job with our company. The interview started out fine, as most interviews do, with exchanging pleasantries and getting to know each other a little bit before launching into the more serious questions. At one point I asked, "How have you responded when you unexpectedly entered a tense situation, either at work or at home?" He started answering the question by telling me that he and his wife just had a new baby, and that they had two other children under the age of five. Exciting and happy news, right? He said that he was under stress because his wife would call his office and say she was going to kill the children. Having been a new mother to two sons (born 15 months apart), I know how wonderful and sometimes stressful being a new mom can be. I empathized with him, and said, "I am so sorry, I know that can be hard, having young children and a new baby. Is she suffering from postpartum depression?" He looked me right in the eyes and said, "No. I am really worried she is going to kill the children." I felt a shiver go through my entire body. At the time, I thought two things: "How horrible and stressful it must be to have his wife call during the day to say she is going to kill the children" and "Oh, my gosh – I can't believe he just shared that with me!"

By asking one very specific question and then listening, I learned more about the person than I ever expected. The purpose of that question is to learn how the candidate responds to and manages stress. What I learned was that this person was under tremendous stress. People cannot perform at their best when they are under high levels of stress at home, and it was clear to me that this candidate needed to spend time at home supporting his wife. It would be best for him and for our company if he didn't have the extra stress of starting a new job at that time.

I was also shocked that he would share something so personal after meeting me just 15 minutes earlier. The fact that he was so transparent in his conversation and revealed something so private told me that he had low EQ. I felt it was inappropriate to share something so intensely personal during a job interview.

When I'm interviewing, I'm not only evaluating whether the person has the hard skills (experience and competency) to do the job, but more importantly, whether they have the soft skills such as warmth, empathy, curiosity, a willingness to learn, and a sense of teamwork. For me, soft skills are always more important than hard skills. You can teach the hard skills – things like Microsoft Office and company-specific tools like Concur and Salesforce – but you can't teach the soft skills. You can't change someone's personality or who they are fundamentally as a human being.

Behavioral interviewing helps you to answer these questions: How well will this candidate fit into our culture? Can they do the work? Will they do the work? What special skills or experience do they bring to the team? Can they take the next job (are they promotable)?

I heard this quote many years ago, and I think it's true: "A people hire A people, B people hire C people, and C people hire losers." The best people in your organization (the A players) have an eye for talent and are always recruiting. They are referring outstanding individuals to the company and growing their own family trees.

Another hiring lesson I've learned is to call the candidate's references personally, always. You want to talk to those people yourself and not rely on someone else to check references. Don't cut corners on reference checking: take the time and perform the due diligence – it will be so worth it.

One of the things my father taught me on our farm was to "prune for better fruit." When he went out to the groves, he would often take me along. Citrus trees require a lot of time, care, and attention, and you must cut back the deadwood to make way for new growth to come in.

Take the time you need to make the right hire, and when you realize that someone is not working out, act quickly and prune for better fruit. Even with all the due diligence, interviewing, and reference checking, sometimes we make a bad hire and early on, we realize we've made a mistake. In my experience, "once a kook, always a kook," and as much as we think we can change someone and "make it work," that's just wishful thinking on our part.

Terminating an employee is never easy. It can be painful – especially when it's dragged out over time. It's like removing a band-aid: do it quickly – it's best for everyone involved. If we're on the wrong path, I like to give feedback early so that the colleague is aware that we are out of step. I think of this feedback as leaving bread crumbs. If the performance does not improve, I provide more feedback – larger than bread crumbs – more like a full loaf of bread, that you could trip over. I believe that a colleague should never be surprised that things are not working out.

We do people a disservice when we "try to make it work" and we both know that it's not the right fit for either of us. We also owe it to our colleague to tell him or her the truth about why it's not working out. Trying to sugarcoat an already difficult situation is disingenuous and doesn't help the employee, who deserves to hear honest feedback. When these conversations are handled with respect, care, and honesty, it's good for everyone. I remember one employee who thanked me. He felt like he had been "set free" to pursue a different career path.

Once you've made an offer and your candidate has accepted, it's time to get everything buttoned down so that they have a very positive onboarding experience. This is an opportunity to put a cherry on top and welcome a new employee to your company in a memorable way. It takes a little bit of effort and planning, but it is so worth it to make the first day special. It's about attention to detail: making sure their desk is clean and stocked with office supplies, a welcome sign, flowers or an orchid, and then taking your new hire to lunch — small things that are thoughtful and unexpected. Together, this simply adds to "the first day of the new job" experience and says, "We're glad you're here, welcome to the team!"

Putting a cherry on top of the onboarding experience means going above and beyond what would normally be expected on the first day of a new job. Not only is it professional to warmly welcome your new employees, but it also reinforces their decision to join your company.

Focus on "the big rocks." Put first things first and hire outstanding talent – and put a cherry on top!

# Cherry on Top #3:
# Culture Always Beats Strategy

I have always valued our people first and foremost. My most important job has always been to show my team my appreciation by making Adecco a great place to work. A huge part of having a great workplace is a thriving culture.

Culture is a word that is difficult to define succinctly. At a workplace, culture is something that can be seen, heard, and felt. If I were asked to draw a picture of "culture" with a piece of plain white paper and a box of crayons, here's what it would look like: an entire page covered from corner to corner with smiley faces of all sizes, shapes, and colors representing happy people with diverse thoughts, experiences, socioeconomic status, beliefs, talents, and backgrounds, working together.

Culture is each of us: what we believe, how we work, and how we interact with each other and our customers. You will know our culture by what we do and say. Our culture is what differentiates us. Our culture is our brand and what others say about our company when we're not in the room. As leaders, we have an awesome responsibility to create, to embrace, and to live our culture. Our culture is what makes us great. It shows the very best of who we are.

As leaders, we have the privilege of creating and protecting our culture. It's not up to Human Resources, Public Relations, Marketing, the CEO, or some other department; it's the individual leader's job. It's your responsibility to create a strong culture.

Create a culture of:

- Integrity: Always doing the right thing
- Rewarding performance
- Support and development
- Communication
- Teamwork and collaboration
- Inclusion
- Hard work and fun

Culture always beats strategy. Having the right culture and the right people is absolutely the most important thing. In his book *The Energy Bus*, Jon Gordon tells us, "Research shows that positive people, positive communication, positive interactions, and positive team cultures produce positive results."

Your culture matters, and you need to protect it like a Fabergé egg. Culture creates engagement – which drives results.

"Engaged people are so much fun to work with, and they deliver great results."
— Patrick De Maeseneire, Former Adecco Group Global CEO

To me, engagement means showing optimism, trust, enthusiasm, love, purpose, joy, passion, and a spirit to live, work, and perform at a high level.

As a leader, I build and lead successful teams by overcoming adversity in my life and at work, showing positivity at all times, sharing contagious energy with colleagues and customers, and bringing out the best in others – and in myself.

Be passionate! Demonstrate engagement and make sure your people feel valued. Your employees need to feel your passion by the things that you say – and believe in your passion by the things that you do. As leaders, we have to work on building relationships with our colleagues, forming trust and making real connections. This is how to put a cherry on top!

Jimmy, a regional vice president, told me one day when we were working together in New Jersey, "A successful leader is a relatable one." I agree. The best leaders must be able to connect with others and they must have the ability to build relationships. As well, people are always watching their leaders for what they say and what they do. A leader's words and actions must align with the company's values: consistency, authenticity, and transparency are key to building and maintaining a robust culture.

Gallup's ongoing study of the future of work is reflected in the book *It's the Manager* by Jim Clifton and Jim Harter, who write, "When you have great managers who can maximize the potential of every team member, you have delivered on the new global will: a great job and a great life."

I have a friend whose son, Brad, is very well-read, articulate, and talented. He is also true to himself, a quality that I admire. Brad lives in San Francisco and has a good job working for a high-profile global company based in London. From my point of view, Brad is successful and has a great job. I can see him staying there for years and being promoted up the ranks. During a conversation, I was telling Brad how I thought he could stay at this company for a long time. I was a bit surprised when he told me, "Joyce, I like what I am doing, but these are not my people." What he meant was that he doesn't feel a connection with the company or the employees he works with. Brad does a great job, but he is probably not fully engaged. For Brad, the culture of the company and the people he works with matter as much as the job.

"The young generation does not want to belong to a company. They want to identify with a purpose. And if they're no longer interested, they leave."
— Alain Dehaze

I recommend learning from the younger generation in your company– and inspiring them. I learned from Brad that his generation is motivated by passion and purpose, and that his personal values must align with the values of the company. He wants to be part of the conversation with other like-minded people, he wants to make a difference, and to have a personal connection with the business.

Listening and learning from millennials helps me to stay relevant and in touch with what our newest members of the workforce want and need from an employer.

How do we do this? As leaders, we must be visible and create an environment where people can do their best work, where employees are seen and heard, and where they believe their contributions are important. Our people are our culture, so always, always, put your people first. Hire the right people, develop them, give them the right leadership – and the right culture. That's the cherry on top.

# Cherry on Top #4:
# Service Never Goes Out of Style

Dance recital in Pompano Beach, FL – 11 years old. I liked winning and getting the trophies!

When my son Coleman was in high school, he was a competitive lacrosse player and earned All-American and All-State honors his senior year. Coleman played attack and faced-off as a midfielder. During his high school career, he scored 131 goals and had 104 assists. He was an aggressive, gritty player who had no quit in him, and at 5'-7" tall, it was always fun to see him running through and by much larger players on his way to firing the ball into the back of the goal.

On a Friday afternoon in the fall of 2008, Coleman had a lacrosse match in the Raleigh-Durham-Chapel Hill area of North Carolina, and I was traveling in the "Triangle" for business. I'd had a super busy day working in the field with our colleagues, running between back-to-back sales appointments and meeting with customers and prospects, but I was determined to get to Coleman's game. I didn't have time for lunch, so by the time I arrived at the AAA five-diamond Umstead Hotel in Cary, North Carolina, I was famished!

After completing the check-in process, the front desk clerk asked me, "Mrs. Russell, is there anything we can do for you this afternoon?" Thinking about how hungry I was, I answered, "Yes, I would love an apple." I just needed something to get me through until I had a chance to eat something more substantial. I was rushing to my room to change my clothes so that I could make it to the match on time. I would have shown up at the field in my work clothes, but a month earlier Coleman asked me if I "could just look like the other moms at the games." I was confused by what he meant by this, so I asked him, and he said, "You know – not in work clothes like you've just come right from the office." It's an amusing dichotomy to be running an almost three-billion-dollar business, and yet rushing to change into jeans, a top, and flats so I don't embarrass my 17-year-old son in front of his high school friends.

I arrived back in the lobby dressed in my "mom outfit," and waiting for me was a hotel server. His arm was bent at a 90-degree angle, and on the palm of his hand rested a silver tray with two apples: one red, and one green. He said, "Mrs. Russell, we didn't know which color you'd prefer." I have repeated this story hundreds of times because it is such a simple story about putting a cherry on top – creating "the wow"! My Umstead Hotel experience is what the cherry on top is all about: an unexpected gesture that expresses thoughtfulness and care. I carried that apple with me to my son's game, and it was a double win that day.

**We are in business to serve people.**
**Leadership is about serving.**

Service never goes out of style. When it comes to products and services, consumers have more choices today than ever before – and service is a clear competitive advantage. Companies like Nordstrom, Ritz-Carlton, Zappos, Southwest Airlines, and grocery stores like Wegmans, Costco, and Publix, understand that service is the heart of everything they do and paramount to their brand and success. Companies with high net promoter scores understand that without a customer, there is no business. Therefore, the client's goals should be at the heart of everything we do. Customers who are appreciated, heard, and know that we are invested in their success are happy and loyal.

During my career, I have flown over a million miles on trips to Europe, Africa, Australia, and the Middle East, and to every major city in the United States. Most of the flights are unremarkable in terms of the experience and the service. When you fly every week, all flights feel the same – unless there is a scary moment, a problem, or a serious delay. In that regard, it's good to have an ordinary flight that is just like all the others, and merely "average." I did have one memorable flight experience with Virgin America Airlines (where I have no special status), and that was because I was given a Cherry on Top service experience.

My colleague, leadership team member, and friend Kristy and I were flying from San Francisco to San Diego for a meeting. Kristy lives in the San Diego area, and I live in Charlotte, so we see each other about four to six times per year, but mainly we speak over the phone. Being on the same flight meant that we'd have time to prepare for the meeting and go over a long list of open items that we needed to discuss. When we compared boarding passes, Kristy was in row eight, and I was in row 16. I approached the gate attendant and explained that my colleague and I were flying together and hoped to get some work done on the plane. I asked if it was possible to change my seat so I could sit next to Kristy. Charlotte is a big hub for American Airlines, and since I rarely book a flight with Virgin America, this was a big "ask," but I thought I would check anyway to see if it could possibly be arranged.

The customer service agent looked at her computer screen, and then went "tap–tap–tap" on the keyboard. I waited patiently and had my fingers crossed for good news. Finally, I heard the printer start to run. She handed me my boarding pass and said, "I have moved your seat to be next to Kristy." I was thrilled that she made the change and that I would be able to sit next to Kristy on the flight. But what she said next was the cherry on top: "I blocked the middle seat for you."

Over the course of the flight, Kristy and I were able to work and get caught up on all our open items and best of all, spend some good quality time together. An unexpected customer service gesture by a helpful airline gate agent gave me the gift of time, the most precious commodity to a leader. It didn't cost anything for the agent to change my seat and block the middle seat. This airline employee was empowered to go above and beyond what is normally expected, and she created "the wow." I could see that it was a joy for her to serve and to have that opportunity to provide exceptional customer service. It's experiences like this that remind me why helpfulness is one of my favorite personality traits. Being nice doesn't take any effort – so go for it! Go out of your way to help others and put a cherry on top. Service never goes out of style.

# Cherry on Top #5: Business is Personal and Relationships Matter

When I started my career with Adecco as a Branch Manager in Charlotte, the only person I knew in the city was David, my new husband of one week and two days. At my new job in "the people business," I was tasked with winning new clients and placing more temporary associates on assignment to work every week. Since I didn't know anyone in Charlotte or have any preexisting relationships, it was up to me to learn the city and the big players/clients in the staffing space.

As a branch manager, my key performance indicators (KPIs) for sales activity were 40 calls per week. These included face-to-face sales presentations by appointment, client calls, and qualifying stops ("Q-stops"). Every Friday afternoon, I was required to submit a weekly sales activity report to my area vice president which detailed all my sales calls for the week. Q-stops involved driving around the city exploring business parks, visiting the largest employers (per the Chamber of Commerce directory), and generally making cold calls on any business that might use staffing services. In my training, I learned that when making a Q-stop, you ask five questions:

#1. Do you use temporary help services? If the answer is "yes," proceed with the following questions:
#2. How many temps are currently working here?
#3. What staffing companies are you currently working with?
#4. Who is the person responsible for making the decision about staffing companies?
#5. Is he/she available to speak to me?

I had been in my new role for only a few months when I spent an afternoon making Q-stops in uptown Charlotte, walking blocks and popping in and out of various companies. On this day, I made a Q-stop that changed my life.

I opened the main door to 201 S. Tryon Street and entered the Barclays American building from the street. To my left was a door that opened into the main reception area for visitors. This small area had a blue carpet, and it reminded me of the reception area in a school principal's office. There were two chairs with a small side table in between, and a woman was sitting behind the reception desk. During sales training, I learned that there are three levels of people at companies who have influence when it comes to selecting staffing companies: the Decision Maker (the person who has the ultimate authority, and the person you want to be dealing with), the Supervisor (someone who supervises temporary associates while they are on assignment), and the Caller (the person who makes the phone calls to place the orders). Seconds after entering the reception area, I made the snap decision that the woman sitting at the desk was the Caller. I assumed she had no decision-making authority.

I approached the desk, and I politely introduced myself. "Hello. My name is Joyce Russell and I'm with Adia Personnel Services." Before I could say anything more, the woman interrupted me, curtly responding, "Do you see that door that you just walked through? Well, you can turn around and walk right back out." I turned around and started for the door, but then I thought, "I need to talk to this woman." So rather than leaving, I turned around, approached her desk and said, "I'm new in Charlotte and I don't know anybody, so do you mind my asking who does your hair?" Almost immediately, the person who two minutes earlier had been irritated with me for dropping in to her work area and had asked me to leave, smiled. We went on to discuss dentists, neighborhoods, favorite stores, and we made a date to have lunch. This conversation was the beginning of one of the most important relationships in my entire career.

Like everyone, Kathy wanted to be seen as a person and approached on a personal level – not just viewed as "the receptionist" and a source of information. You see, Kathy wasn't the "Caller" as I had initially assumed; she had major influence at Barclays and was part of the team of Decision Makers. And like all of us, she wanted to be seen, to be heard, and to be appreciated. This was the moment in my career that I began to understand that meaningful connections between people are important.

During our lunch, Kathy gave me an order for a Wang word processor secretary. In the late eighties, Wang word processors were in high demand, and the good ones were kept busy. I knew that Kathy was testing me with her first order; she wanted to see if I could deliver. If we did a good job on this order, more orders would follow. And that's exactly what happened. We slowly earned the right to more and more business. Kathy was a tough customer; she always expected only the highest-quality associates, and if a temp wasn't working out, she was quick to pick up the phone and tell me about it – she expected me to fix the problem ASAP. Failure was not an option.

Not only did we provide Barclays American with Cherry on Top service, but I also worked very hard to build my relationship with Kathy. At least once a month, Kathy and I had lunch, always going to her favorite place – the restaurant at the Radisson Hotel, which was downtown and close to her office. During one lunch, Kathy shared with me her love of professional basketball and specifically, Michael Jordan. 1988 was the inaugural season of the Charlotte Hornets, and the town was buzzing about this new basketball team. Most games were sold out, with enthusiastic Charlotteans who embraced their first professional team filling the seats. Attending a Charlotte Hornets game was an event, and for the "big games," everyone in town wanted to be there.

When it was announced that Charlotte would be getting an NBA expansion team, my husband David jumped at the chance to buy season tickets. David has always loved basketball. For the past 12 years, he has served as the assistant coach of the girls' basketball team at Providence Day in Charlotte, winning nine state championships. David also referees college games, having worked his way up from reffing high school games.

This was during the late 1980s when there was no bigger name in all of sports than Michael Jordan. Having played college ball for the University of North Carolina–Chapel Hill, MJ is very popular in Charlotte. So you can imagine that when my husband found out that Michael Jordan was coming to town with Scottie Pippen and Horace Grant to face the Hornets led by Muggsy Bogues, Kelly Tripucka, and Dell Curry (now known as "Steph's Dad"), David wanted to be in our seats at the Charlotte Coliseum. It was an act of love that David gave up our seats so I could give our tickets to Kathy. Knowing that he would have other opportunities to see Michael Jordan and the other top players of the time like Charles Barkley, Magic Johnson, Isiah Thomas, Karl Malone, and Larry Bird, David showed an "abundance mentality" in giving up the tickets. Kathy never expected to go to the Hornets-Bulls game. For her, it was a Cherry on Top experience to see Michael Jordan play in Charlotte. I am pretty sure Kathy told everyone she knew every detail about being at the game that night watching Michael Jordan play.

Over time, we earned more and more business with Barclays American, and they grew to be one of our top customers. It was through my relationship with Kathy that I learned about another opportunity that would take my career to the next level. Barclays American Mortgage was expanding in Charlotte, and Kathy introduced me to their top decision-makers. Every staffing company in Charlotte was competing for this business. Thanks to Kathy, we "got our foot in the door," and, during the peak period of their business, we had 300 temporary associates working there! Business is personal, and relationships do matter!

Another one of my favorite relationship stories started with a conversation about The Oprah Winfrey Show. A very good friend, Mandy, who was also a customer, told me it was her lifelong dream to see Oprah live in Chicago. For Mandy, being an audience member at Oprah's show was a "bucket list" item. Since its debut, Oprah was the number one talk show, and for many years, the highest-rated program in daytime television. With fewer than 300 seats per taping, though, getting a ticket to the show was next to impossible.

A few weeks later, I was in my office talking with my friend and colleague Scott, who worked on our national accounts team as an account manager. I had known Scott for a long time. We worked together on several accounts, and we had a great working relationship. I was telling Scott about my conversation with Mandy and how much she wanted to go to the Oprah show, but how hard it was to get tickets. Without missing a beat, Scott said, "I can get tickets to Oprah." I responded in disbelief: "What? You can? How?" He said, "My brother works as an executive vice president for ABC in Chicago, and he can get tickets." I was floored and delighted by this news. Scott, true to his word, came through with two tickets to The Oprah Winfrey Show.

People are the source of key assets, opportunities, and information. If it hadn't been for my relationship with Scott, we never would have checked off Oprah on Mandy's bucket list. In the fall of 2006, Mandy and I planned our trip to Chicago.

When the big day arrived, we queued up to enter Harpo Studios. It was a cold day in the windy city in late October, but the excitement and energy kept us warm. Once we were inside the building, the line moved up and down and back and forth, reminiscent of a highly organized ride line at Disney World. While we waited, previous Oprah shows were being shown on the screens overhead. I think everyone there was secretly hoping this would be an "Oprah's Favorite Things" show, and we'd all leave the studio with our arms filled with beautiful clothes, jewelry, and the latest tech gadget. As it turned out, this episode was better than that.

Oprah's guests that day were Earvin "Magic" Johnson and his wife Cookie. Fifteen years earlier, Earvin had retired from the NBA after being diagnosed with HIV. Watching them from my seat in the studio, I was amazed at their openness and honesty as they talked with Oprah. From the affection Earvin and Cookie shared for one another, I could see they were a solid, dedicated team. In person, Earvin is exactly as you see him on TV: he is a warm, genuine, super-engaging, and positive human being.

Coincidentally, just 10 days before he appeared on Oprah, Earvin had been the keynote speaker at the National Minority Supplier Development Council Conference. Earvin talked about the importance of diversity in hiring and making investments in underserved communities. Adecco's vice president of supplier diversity was in the audience. She had met with Kawanna Brown, the COO of Magic Johnson Enterprises, and they had started building a relationship and talking about ways that Adecco and Magic Johnson Enterprises could work together.

Fast forward to the end of the Oprah show. As the show wrapped and Earvin and Cookie were leaving the stage, they walked right in front of where Mandy and I were sitting. I reached out my hand and said, "Hello, Mr. Johnson, I'm Joyce Russell, president and COO of Adecco." Earvin stopped in his tracks, grabbed my hand, and with his huge, megawatt smile said, "Joyce Russell, I have been wanting to meet you."

After more than a year of meetings, conference calls, and back and forth between executives and attorneys, Adecco entered into a strategic alliance with Magic Workforce Solutions, a newly created minority-owned staffing company. At a rooftop party in Manhattan with a view of St. Patrick's Cathedral, together with MWS, Adecco launched our new venture in September 2008.

I believe success in sales depends upon building trust before solutions can be proposed and accepted. Trust only develops when a relationship is strong.

Through our many meetings and conversations, we built strong relationships with Earvin and Kawanna that resulted in a brand-new strategic alliance between Magic Johnson Enterprises and Adecco.

Meaningful connections between people are important.

We had the honor of hosting Earvin in 2007 when he spoke at our annual kick-off meeting, Adecco's Leadership Summit in Orlando, Florida. He spoke right before our last speaker for the day. Earvin shared his personal, business, and Los Angeles Laker stories with our colleagues, and he was magnanimous with his time. He was warm, funny, and engaging as he regaled us with tales of competing against Larry Bird and Michael Jordan. Although his time had run out, Earvin wanted to take questions from our colleagues. Due to the imminent airport departures for 500+ people in the audience, we had to inform our final speaker (who was waiting backstage and whom we had already paid to speak for one hour) that we didn't have time left on the agenda for him. The speaker wasn't happy, but we offered our sincere apologies. Our colleagues were thrilled to have met Earvin "Magic" Johnson, and they left the national meeting fired-up and ready to get to work!

Relationships can help you grow your business and they can be instrumental in solving problems. Many times throughout the course of my career, having a strong relationship with someone has helped me to resolve a serious business issue. One of the most memorable examples of this had to do with a worker's compensation rate problem with a state government agency.

As an employer, Adecco is responsible for all payroll taxes, including state and federal taxes, unemployment tax, and worker's compensation. These rates vary from state to state, and in addition to the pay rate, they are part of the hourly bill rate we charge our clients. When there is an increase in any payroll tax, we must pass along the incremental cost to the client. Since taxes are a real cost associated with our business, what seems to be a minor rate issue can be huge in terms of dollars and profit margins.

We had a large contract with a southern state, and we received notification that the worker's compensation rates were increasing for the following year. The contract did not allow for bill rate increases during the term of the contract because of changes in tax rates. Our margins on this account were very thin. If we were unable to pass through the taxes with an increase to our hourly bill rates (to adjust for the new higher worker's comp rates), the account would be marginally profitable. Since we don't provide our services for free, I had to find a solution.

The local and regional teams were aware of the problem

and were working on possible ideas, but dealing with state governments can be cumbersome, and we needed a solution fast. We had worked with this client for many years, and we wanted to continue our long relationship – yet we had to make a profit.

During this time, I was attending a Committee of 200 ("C200") event. C200 is a close-knit group of accomplished women leaders who support and inspire each other and develop the next generation of women leaders. I've been a member of C200 for more than 10 years, and I've met many wonderful women and developed close relationships with my C200 "sisters." During this particular event, I reconnected with one of my C200 friends, Susan. She and I went for a power walk, and I told her about the business problem we had with the state and the worker's comp rates. I was hoping that Susan might have some ideas or advice for me that would help me work through the issue. After I went through the long explanation of the problem, Susan didn't miss a beat. "Sugar," she said, "that's not a problem at all. I am friends with the governor." The following week, Susan sent me a note letting me know that the governor would be calling my office. About an hour later, my wonderful executive assistant, Ansley, (my rock for 15 years) placed a phone call on hold and said, "Joyce, the governor's office is on the line."

I proceeded to have a very cordial and professional conversation with the governor. I explained the issue and proposed a solution. He said, "Joyce, thank you for bringing this to my attention. I will look into this, and someone from my office will be getting back to you." A week later, the entire problem had been resolved with a positive outcome for Adecco and the state – truly a "win-win."

Here is another story about meaningful connections that produce results. In the staffing industry, we often enter into contracts and agreements with managed service providers (MSPs). Some large companies outsource the management of their contingent labor to an MSP that takes on the role of managing all the staffing vendors in the client's program.

In 2018, we won a large piece of business with a national retail company. We had worked on this deal for several years, and we were delighted about the win! As is sometimes the case when a contract is being negotiated and bounces back and forth between companies, we hit a snag on the contract language. We arrived at an impasse. Unless the problem with the contract language could be changed to the satisfaction of both parties, we would not be moving forward with the multi-million-dollar deal.

When I heard this news, I reached out to my friend Steve, who was an executive with the MSP company managing the contract. I said, "Steve, we have a problem, and I need your help." I explained the problem with the contract language and the concerns raised by our legal team. Steve listened and acknowledged that he understood the problem, and then he said, "Joyce, thank you for letting me know. Stay tuned – I'll take care of it." A very short time later, an email arrived in my inbox from Mark, my colleague on the Adecco side leading the sale.

September 14, 2018 10:13 AM
To: Russell, Joyce
Subject: FW: Please DocuSign: AGS @ Supplier Agreement
Good Morning,
We all of a sudden seem to have resolution on the Agreement cap language. I will be routing this for signature internally as soon as they send over the final. Thank you all for your help on this, and especially Joyce for connecting with Steve.
Regards,
Mark

Having meaningful relationships with people is not just about business. It's about getting to know people and making real connections with them. It's about building friendships and having a circle of people on whom you can rely and trust. And, it's about knowing when it is appropriate to leverage your relationships, and when it's not. You should have the emotional intelligence to know when you can ask a favor of someone, and when the favor would be too much to ask. You do not want to put someone you have built trust with into an uncomfortable situation. You also need to know when it's time to reciprocate, and how best to do that.

Through C200 and other organizations, I have a network of people that I can count on because I have made the effort and the investment of time to make connections and to build these strong relationships.

When we are competing for large contracts, I am always disappointed if I hear from the lead salesperson, "We lost on price." What that really means to me is that we didn't have a relationship. Your ability to build, maintain, and leverage meaningful relationships is critical to your success and to achieving your goals. Building relationships with the right people creates a larger sphere of influence. That is the cherry on top.

During the last 10 years of my career, I began to truly understand the value of investing in and mentoring the next generation of leaders. This is something that I have enjoyed immensely as I've shared my experiences and relationships with others. It's been such a joy for me to open doors for friends and bring people into conversations through my relationships. I think of it this way: when I introduce someone, I am "putting my name" on that person, and some of my credibility rubs off of me and is transferred to the person whom I am introducing.

Making the effort and taking the time to share my relationships and create opportunities for others has been a cherry on top for me!

A few final thoughts to leave you with:

- Meaningful connections between people are important.
- People are your sources for key assets, opportunities, and information.
- Business is personal and relationships do matter!

# Cherry on Top #6: Retention of People Has a Direct Correlation to Profit

As I said in Chapters One and Two, the most important part of every organization is its people. In Chapter Three, I talked about the importance of having a strong and supportive organizational culture that matches up with the wants and needs of the employees. The secret to success is hiring, training, and developing the best people, having a great culture, and retaining your top performers. Retention of your people has a direct correlation to profit.

A study by The Center for American Progress[1] found that turnover costs are often estimated to be 100% to 300% of the base salary of a replaced employee, depending on the wage and the role of the employee. On average, the costs to replace an employee are:

- 20% of annual salary for mid-range positions (earning $30,000 to $50,000 a year).
- Up to 213% of annual salary for highly-compensated executive positions.

Turnover is expensive in many ways. You have to factor in the hard and soft costs of separation, recruiting/hiring/ training, lost productivity, impact on morale, and loss of knowledge – the "brain drain" that occurs when tenured talented people leave your company.

So, how do we ensure that we retain talent? The first step is hiring people who are a good fit for your company; people who not only have the skills to do the job, but who also fit

---

[1] Boushey, H. and Glynn, S. "There are Significant Business Costs to Replacing Employees," White Paper, Center for American Progress, November 16, 2012

into your culture. Making good hires and selecting talent is job Number One. In *Good to Great*, Jim Collins writes, "In fact, leaders of companies that go from good to great start not with 'where' but with 'who.' They start by getting the right people on the bus, the wrong people off the bus, and the right people in the right seats." I love this idea. I believe that people are happiest and do their best work when they are working from their strengths and are in "the right seats on the bus."

I have seen firsthand that high levels of employee engagement greatly increase retention and decrease turnover. People want to feel special, to be seen, to be heard, and to be understood. Employees stay where they are paid well, mentored, challenged, promoted, involved, appreciated, valued, on a mission, empowered, and trusted. Employees want an employer who is as invested in them as they are in the company. They are looking for a relationship versus a transaction.

Studies have shown that leaders who demonstrate high levels of "personal warmth" have a better chance at long-term success.
— Loran Nordgren, The Kellogg School

Reward the doers: invest in your high performers and help them to develop and grow. At our citrus groves, Dad had a regular watering and fertilizing schedule to keep the trees healthy and producing high-quality fruit. Like Dad, I believe in "sprinkling fertilizer"—on your people. I view training and development opportunities as an investment in their growth.

I was fortunate to attend many outstanding training programs during my career, and one of my favorites was Harvard Law School's Program on Negotiation. After attending the program, I felt more confident about getting a good outcome during negotiations because of what I had learned. One of my favorite exercises involved an orange. We worked in pairs at our table, and the challenge for my partner Alex and me was to negotiate for the whole orange. The twist to the exercise was that we were not allowed to explain the reason that we wanted the orange. For the next 15 minutes, we engaged in an animated conversation, each making our passionate case for the orange.

At the end of the negotiation, Alex and I agreed that the best thing to do was to cut the orange in half. At face value, this appears to be a "win-win," but as it turns out, neither of us was happy with the outcome; in fact, we were both disappointed. During the discussion that followed, I revealed that I wanted the orange because I needed the peel to zest for my carrot cake recipe. And, Alex told me that he needed the juice from the orange to make an exotic drink. If I had been able to determine the reason Alex wanted the whole orange (what the real value was for him) I would have proposed a different solution during the negotiation: I would take the entire orange peel and Alex could have the whole orange. In a negotiation, both parties are wanting something, and you have to find out what that is. What is your goal in the negotiation, and how can both parties get what they want?

After attending the three-day class and fully absorbing all the information I learned, I realized that my company had made an investment in me by sending me to that class in Cambridge. I learned a new set of interpersonal tools and strategies, and I felt more confident in negotiations. Having that extra fertilizer spread on me was a psychological raise. It was a cherry on top – something unexpected yet special that added to my experience as a colleague and deepened my sense of loyalty to my company

Loyalty is an emotional connection. Employees of companies with strong corporate cultures wear their company t-shirts and have a feeling of pride and loyalty about who they work for. That emotional connection is made by helping other people to grow, by creating experiences, and by voting with your time. Maya Angelou said, "I've learned that people will forget what you said, people will forget what you did, but people will never forget how you made them feel." Fundamentally, all of us want to feel special and appreciated. Our strongest memories (both the good and the bad) are those moments in our lives where we had a strong emotional connection to an event. That's why I strongly believe in creating superlative experiences for people. When you share an experience with your co-workers, you form a bond and create shared memories. And you inspire loyalty.

Every year, we recognize and celebrate our top performers at our Superstars event. This special event is held at a different location each year. One year, we were in New Orleans and we had our own Mardi Gras street parade. But my most vivid memory is of our sunrise balloon trip in Aspen, Colorado. Although everyone had to get up super early, it was such an incredible experience to see the sun rise over the mountains, and then to be served a champagne breakfast upon landing.

The possibilities are limitless. Whether it's a nighttime tour of the monuments in Washington, DC, a carriage ride to dinner in Charleston, South Carolina, a Cirque du Soleil show, or planting 50 pink flamingos in a front yard to celebrate an employees' birthday, it's important to create experiences and memories. So go ahead, put a cherry on top. Dare to be different!

The best experience I've had as an Adecco colleague, hands down, was when I was honored by being selected as a Torch Runner for the 2000 Summer Olympic Games in Sydney, Australia. Through the years, Adecco has been involved with the Olympic Games, helping to staff some of the events around the world and supporting Olympic athletes through the U.S. Olympic and Paralympic Committee's Athlete Career and Education program. In 2000, one male and one female colleague from Adecco in the United States were selected to represent the company and carry the torch in the days leading up to the opening ceremony on September 15. Colleagues in other countries around the world were included as well. The cherry on top was that Adecco invited David and our two sons, Bryson and Coleman, to make the trip with me across the world to Australia, and it was extra special that my Mom, Dad, and two sisters shared the experience with me as well.

Being an Olympic Games torch runner is not as easy as it looks. First, the torch weighs 3.5 pounds, and second, each leg of the torch relay is one mile. Since I had been doing more Adecco work than working out, I decided I'd better train and get into shape. My training regimen included running while holding a five-pound bag of sugar up over my shoulder by my ear. For a month, I made regular trips to a park close to my home to run around the small fishing pond with a bag of sugar. I had to be ready to run while carrying the torch, to represent Adecco and make my family proud.

In the days leading up to our departure, I envisioned myself running along a dusty road through the Australian Outback with kangaroos and dingoes. As it turned out, that was not the case. I was thrilled when I learned I would be running in Sydney on the day prior to the Opening Ceremony. The torch relay had begun in Olympia, Greece on May 10, and after more than four months and 22,000 miles, the torch would be handed off to me. I would be carrying the flame that would light the cauldron in the Olympic Stadium and mark the start of the Games the following day.

The best part of the entire experience, the cherry on top, was having my family with me. The most memorable moment for me happened as I was running down the middle of the street, between police officers on motorcycles. The sidewalks were filled with people cheering as I ran by with the torch in one hand, and I waved with the other. Through all the adrenaline, excitement, and noise, I heard Coleman shouting, "That's my mother! That's my mother!" It is a moment I will cherish forever.

Experiences like this bring people together, create memories, and build lasting relationships. Strong relationships drive job satisfaction, engagement, and retention. Because people work for people. They don't work for companies. People don't quit companies – they quit people. And when people leave, they are quitting their direct manager. 75% of people who voluntarily quit their job are quitting their boss, according to a Gallup analysis. Work relationships take work; they must be built over time and closely managed.

One way that I remain cognizant of my relationships is by using what Stephen Covey calls The Emotional Bank Account.

The Emotional Bank Account is a brilliant concept that reminds us to be aware of both our positive and negative interactions with others. Think of your Emotional Bank Account in the same way that you think of your checking account: your total deposits must be greater than your total withdrawals, or you will be quickly overdrawn ("in the negative"). You will then find yourself in a stressful situation that could have been avoided with a little attention, care, and diligence. In all of our relationships (as a leader, friend, boss, mother/father, wife/husband/partner), sometimes we must have difficult conversations and make hard decisions that may not be popular or well-received.

Communicating to a direct report that their annual salary increase is less than what they'd expected, having a tough conversation with your teenager about grades, accidentally hurting your spouse's feelings by something you said, being late to meet a friend for dinner – these are examples of "withdrawals" from The Emotional Bank

Account. When too many of these "withdrawals" add up, we quickly become "overdrawn" from those whom we care most about. Colleagues who feel their manager is overdrawn in his or her Emotional Bank Account are less engaged, less productive, and more likely to be looking for a new opportunity outside of the company.

That's why we must be mindful of the power of our words. What we do and what we say impacts others. This is part of having high emotional intelligence, "EQ": being self-aware enough to know how to manage our Emotional Bank Account with others. Making deposits into someone's Emotional Bank Account is the easy part. Simple gestures like writing a heartfelt, handwritten thank-you note, praising a colleague in front of his/her peers at a meeting, decorating a colleague's office for their birthday, telling your son/daughter that you are proud of them and why, helping a neighbor with a project, calling an old friend to catch-up, surprising your husband/wife/partner with tickets to see their favorite band, and the list goes on. I'm sure you can think of spectacular examples! Making deposits in someone's Emotional Bank Account involves going above and beyond to put a cherry on top, letting people know how much they are valued, appreciated, and loved.

How you show up with your people every day is super important and has a direct impact on retention. Your reputation follows you and builds year after year. You can spot true leaders by the things they say and the things they do; you can tell who is a true leader by their actions. Think about how it feels to work with a moody, irritable, or otherwise unhappy manager. That is not the environment in which people aspire to do their best work. As a leader, you set the tone. People are watching you and listening to your words, and your team members become a direct reflection of you. The higher you go up in an organization, the higher your EQ needs to be. From my experience, your first promotion is based on 90% IQ (what you know) and 10% EQ (how you relate to others). Your second promotion is evenly balanced at 50% - 50%, and your third promotion is based on 20% IQ and 80% EQ. The most powerful leadership tool you have is your own personal example.

Several years ago, my friend Joanie shared an article from Inc. magazine written by Bill Carmody, CEO of Trepoint. In the article, Bill explained his idea of "The Lifeline," a simple idea that illustrates that for any situation or problem, we can choose our approach. We can take the attitude of an empowered person or we can play the role of victim.

Figure 1 – The Lifeline

| The Lifeline | |
|---|---|
| **Powerful / Accountable** | **Powerless / Victim** |
| 8 – Make It Happen | 4 – Wait & Hope |
| 7 – Find Solutions | 3 – Excuse: "I Can't" |
| 6 – "Own It" | 2 – Blame Others |
| 5 – Acknowledge Reality | 1 – Unaware & Unconscious |

Do you recognize yourself or others in some of these statements? We all know people who under stress default to the right-hand column – they make excuses, blame others, play the victim, or they are simply unaware and unconscious.

I prefer to work with people who, in stressful situations, respond on the left side; these people are powerful and accountable. They say things like, "I own this" or "I've got this," and they make things happen. They find solutions and they acknowledge reality – they have high EQ! You can recognize powerful and accountable leaders by the things they say and the things they do. As a leader, exhibiting behaviors on the right side (Powerless/Victim) of the table is the danger zone; my advice is to stay left!

Your leadership traits and behaviors will make your reputation as a leader – positive or negative. Leadership is really about your ability to bring people along with you. I've heard it said that, "Leadership is about followership, so turn around and see if anybody is there." Building a followership not only impacts your reputation as a leader, but also helps to build culture, loyalty, retention – and your business.

We know that employees feel a connection with their company when they are involved, consulted, and heard. Town hall style gatherings, monthly and quarterly all-colleague calls, Google hangouts, Skype, and Webex meetings all help to drive higher levels of employee communication and engagement.

But I believe that the best way to show people that you care about them is to spend time with them. As leaders, the most precious commodity we have is time. In both our personal and professional lives, we vote with our time.

The most meaningful and generous gift we can give someone is to take time out of our crazy, hectic schedules to be fully present with them, and vote with our time.

Here is a short list of my advice for creating a happy workplace and a positive culture where employees can grow and thrive:

- Leadership is about serving. It is a joy to serve, and we are in business to serve people.
- Go out of your way to help others.
- Treat everybody like a customer.
- Be positive and optimistic, no matter what – attitude can outshine aptitude.
- Have an "attitude of latitude:" it's okay to make mistakes.
- Be happy or be gone.
- Be present and be willing to make personal sacrifices, to be inconvenienced, and accessible and available to others – do not exhibit signs of Vitamin B ("Being Present") deficiency!
- Over-communicate.
- Play ping–pong: Take time to listen and bounce ideas back and forth and include people in decision-making.
- Know what motivates people. Not everyone is motivated by the same things; treat everyone as an individual.
- Remember, there are no perfect people.
- Leverage strengths.
- Care more and settle for more – complacency is dangerous.
- You are losing if you make it confusing.
- Use what you know to create delight – to put a cherry on top.

The definition of leadership is followership—
so look behind you to see if anybody is there.

Meaningful connections between colleagues create vibrant culture. As a leader, when you like and respect the people you work with and show that you care, you drive employee engagement and retention. Strong bonds between colleagues at all levels of the company elevate the performance of employees and ultimately, your profit.

Build loyalty, create experiences, make tiny changes, vote with your time, manage the Emotional Bank Accounts between yourself and others. And always, put a cherry on top!

# Cherry on Top #7: Go to the Fire

In the first part of this book, I talked about talent, the importance of people, and the impact that your colleagues have on your company or organization. I shared my thoughts about culture and retention, why they are important, and how they contribute to your success. Leaders who have "an eye for talent" have an edge because having the ability to identify, recruit, hire, train, and develop special people is the difference between winning and losing.

Having the guts to make the tough decisions and handle confrontation are other "must-have" skills of a successful leader. These are sometimes the hardest skills for a leader to learn – especially a new leader. During many conversations with members of my senior leadership team, we would be discussing issues concerning their direct reports, and I'd ask, "Well, did you confront him/her on that? Or, "Have you had a serious conversation about that?" And many times the answer was, "No. Not yet, but I will."

Here are the reasons those conversations usually do not take place: confrontation is scary, it's hard, and it's uncomfortable – and most people are chicken. We have a high need to be liked, and to have warm, friendly relationships with our people. We want others to speak positively about us, and we want to have a good reputation. When we confront someone, it can feel like we're putting all of that at risk. But the fact of the matter is that confrontation means you care, and that's why you need to "go to the fire."

My Dad once told me, "If people don't like you, they ignore you." Good leaders confront people because they do care; because they are genuinely concerned about that person and want to help to make them better. We are doing people a disservice when we don't tell them the truth. When you have difficult conversations, when you go to the fire, you are telling that person, "I care enough to confront you."

Just as parents have a responsibility to raise their children, leaders have an awesome responsibility to develop and "raise" the people in their care. Sometime during my sons' high school years, my mother told me, "Joyce, you're only as happy as your most unhappy child." Mom was right. I have found her theory to be true at home and at work. Children want and need structure, discipline, and feedback, and the same is true of the people we work with. We have to learn to communicate and give feedback – both the good and the bad – even when it's hard.

Learning to go to the fire is an acquired skill, one that must be developed and practiced. Confrontation doesn't come naturally to most people, so it's something you must work at and improve over time. Being able to have tough conversations is something that I had to learn as a leader. Trust me, the more you do it, the easier it becomes to go to the fire. It's not about being tough or hard on your people. Remember, at its core, going to the fire means that you care about your people, and that you have the guts to have open and honest conversations with them.

I remember one of my most difficult conversations. It was with a member of my team who had many wonderful qualities: smart, tremendous work ethic, customer-focused, attention to detail, articulate, driven, ambitious, and hard-charging. It was the last piece, hard-charging, that led to problems with her people. In my experience, being "too hard-charging" shows up as being tough on your people, and that is usually not a good thing.

When managers are tough on their employees, this is what their employees believe: "These expectations are unrealistic, nothing is ever good enough, I can never measure up, I am inadequate, overly criticized, and underappreciated."

I did like that Caroline was a "pusher," that she drove for results, that she had high standards, but what I didn't like was that this was done at the expense of her direct reports. The problem was that Caroline was completely unaware of four things: her people were unhappy, they didn't like working for her, they were at risk of leaving the company (some had already left), and her management style was holding her back from being promoted.

Unfortunately, Caroline was not self-aware enough (there's the EQ again) to realize that her team members were unhappy and quitting her. Many were disengaged, and some were actively looking for positions outside the company. I was hearing about the problems directly from Caroline's team members, and indirectly through others. I had a choice: I could ignore it and hope the problem would go away, or I could go to the fire. I chose to go to the fire.

It is never easy having a difficult conversation, but we owe it to our people and the company to let people know when they are not performing at their best. At the outset, there are two things required for a positive and productive "go to the fire" conversation: trust and transparency. At the beginning of my meeting with Caroline, I told her, "I need to have a difficult conversation with you." In a very open and honest way, I told Caroline about the feedback I had received about her management style. I explained that although I appreciated her work ethic and sense of urgency, being too tough on her people was holding her back in her career.

The natural inclination of people during these conversations is to be defensive, so I gave Caroline specific examples of situations where her colleagues felt diminished, and I explained the impact of her words and her actions on her team. Sometimes, leaders aren't aware of the impact their words, tone of voice, and use of sarcasm or humor have on others.

As well, people with low EQ often overestimate the state of their relationships and are unaware of how others actually see them. I explained that my goal is always to set up people for success, not failure. I clearly outlined why this problem was keeping Caroline from advancing, and if she didn't become a better "people leader," she would not be considered for the next role, something she desperately aspired to. I also shared my own challenges with being too hard on people because of unrealistic expectations, and I told Caroline how I had learned from those mistakes. At the end of our conversation, I said, "You can trust me to work with you, or you can take the problem somewhere else. I have your best interest at heart, and I want you to be successful." Transparency and vulnerability are bonding. Be open and honest with people and share your own struggles and challenges.

It is hard for people to change. And it's especially difficult to change one's management style after operating in the same mode for years and getting away with it. I knew that this was going to be a challenge for Caroline and that it would take time and work. To help her in this process, I offered to hire a professional coach for her – someone who was outside the company she could talk to, and who could help her become a better, more effective leader. As hard as it was for me to have this conversation with Caroline, I know I did the right thing. She later thanked me for telling her the truth. In the end, that's what everyone wants.

The cherry on top of "going to the fire" is taking the extra time and care to confront your people with specific information about what is holding them back, to make investments in them, and to help them achieve their full potential as colleagues, leaders, contributors, and human beings.

Confrontation means you care.

We have a responsibility to hold people accountable for what we need them to do. Lack of accountability creates complacency, and complacency leads to nowhere good. That's why I encourage you to "inspect what you expect." If your team members have key performance indicators (KPIs), you must review reports or dashboards regularly to understand who is achieving the numbers, who is exceeding, and who is falling short of the goals. If performance is based on budget, then monthly and quarterly meetings are necessary to determine where you are, where you need to get to, and how you will get there. People need and want direction, guidance, and feedback – and that's your job. Our colleagues can't do their best when they don't know what is expected of them. I like to outline exactly what is required to "get an A" and *how* to achieve high marks.

I wasn't always this way. When I was an area vice president, I had an annoying habit I was unaware of until one of my branch managers, Sarah, pointed it out. All branch managers had goals for monthly sales and profit. The sales were driven by the number of hours you billed, the number of temporary associates your branch had working at client companies. Quite frequently, I would say to Sarah, "You need to get your hours up," and Sarah would say, "Joyce, I know." What I didn't realize at the time was that I was telling Sarah *what* she had to do to make her goals, but not *how* to do it. I was stating the obvious without giving any clear direction about how to achieve the goal.

That became an "aha moment" for me, when I realized that Sarah needed my help and guidance on how to increase the revenue in her branch. From that time forward, every week we made sales calls together. We scheduled a specific day (or two) that we would work together, and it was my expectation that she would have appointments booked with decision-makers at prospect companies. Before every sales call, we would talk about the objective of the appointment, and then right after the call we would debrief on what went well, what could be improved, and the next steps that required follow-up. There was usually a lunch appointment during the day, and that time was spent building relationships with current clients or prospects. At the end of every day, Sarah wrote thank-you notes and set up more appointments for the following week. I would look forward to the days we spent together, and I was always happy when we came away from meetings with new orders. Sarah's hours went up, and that year she became one of five Adia colleagues to earn the new title, senior branch manager.

Holding people accountable for what they are supposed to do means you "hold their feet to the fire." You create a sense of urgency about accomplishing goals. But most importantly, you don't simply tell them; you show them. You teach people how to do their jobs. Telling Sarah that she needed to "get her hours up" wasn't helpful – she already knew that. What was helpful and productive was working with Sarah side by side, investing my time in her and showing and teaching her how to make successful sales calls that generated new orders and revenue for her branch.

Confrontation and tough conversations are stressful; it's never easy. I know I spent many sleepless nights tossing and turning, worried about having to speak with someone the next day to deliver a difficult message. I had to remind myself that ignoring the problem would only cause the person to fail, and that "confrontation means you care."

One way that I make these situations a little easier is by using the "Oreo Cookie" approach. When I was a little girl, I loved Oreo cookies, especially with a glass of milk, right after school. Like many children (and adults), my favorite way to eat them was to carefully separate the two chocolate cookies on the outside so I could get to the good stuff – the cream filling on the inside. It helps me when I am going to the fire to start the conversation with something positive – that's one of the chocolate cookies. You can always find something nice to say about someone, so I make a point of sincerely complimenting the person on something they do exceptionally well. Our goal is not to beat up on someone and point out all their shortcomings, but rather to get to the cream filling and talk about the specific problem or issue. After we've given the feedback in an honest and clear way, we close the conversation with the other half of the cookie, again pointing out areas where the colleague does a super job and excels in their role, focusing on the positives. Using the Oreo Cookie method has made it easier for me to have difficult conversations, and I hope less stressful for the person receiving the message.

There are no perfect people, but there are special people in our lives, at work and at home. One of the joys in life, a cherry on top, is that we have the privilege to care for them, to make a difference, and to ensure that they grow and thrive.

# Cherry on Top #8:
# Your Boss is Your Best Customer

Up to now, we've been focused on hiring top-notch talent, sparking employee engagement, building culture, driving retention, and managing relationships with your employees and clients. All of these are paramount for high-performing teams and organizations, and especially for your success as a leader. Having the best numbers and an impeccable reputation inside and outside of your company, and being known as "a star," are very important factors in building your career. But there is one relationship that should be top of mind: your relationship with your boss. Everything else can be great – you can be a top performer, a subject matter expert, and you can have an important title and a ton of responsibility – but if you don't have a good relationship with your boss, nothing else matters.

It's up to you to manage your relationship with your boss. This is arguably the most important relationship you have at work. And you "own" that; not your boss or direct manager, not human resources or another team member, but y-o-u.

A few years ago, I was having lunch with a friend, and he told me, "I love my job, but I hate my boss." My immediate reaction to this statement was "danger-danger-danger!" I am very intuitive, and I had sensed that Cliff was miserable and was seeking my advice. He liked the company; he had worked there for almost 20 years, and he could see himself staying there until he retired in 10 years. I knew that unless Cliff worked on his relationship with his manager, he might not make it there 90 more days.

Cliff continued to tell me the myriad of reasons he didn't

like his boss, including that he could no longer leave the office before 5 pm to coach the girl's soccer team at the local college – something he had done for years. Cliff is passionate about coaching, and missing that activity felt like a huge withdrawal from Cliff's Emotional Bank Account. After patiently listening to all of his complaints, I said, "Cliff, if you don't like your boss, she probably doesn't like you, either." Silence. Complete and utter silence from someone who was rarely at a loss for words. It never occurred to Cliff that if you don't like someone, there's a good chance they feel the exact same way about you. At that point, I had Cliff's full attention.

I said, "Cliff, you own your relationship with your boss. It's up to you to make it better. It's not your boss' responsibility to change. You have to adapt and figure out how you can work together. If you're miserable, trust me, so is she." I explained to Cliff that he had a choice: he could choose to ignore the problem and stay, in which case he would probably be replaced in the next year, or he could stay and work on his relationship with his boss. I think it was beginning to sink in with Cliff that this was something that he had to fix, and he was the one who had to do the work. From there, we talked about various strategies for improving his relationship, including suggesting that he get into work earlier in the morning so that leaving by 5 pm was not an issue. It took time, but slowly, Cliff's relationship with his boss improved. He later told me that he took ownership of the problem and fixed the relationship by changing the focus from himself to his boss and what was important to her.

In most professions and industries, there are people and customers with whom we don't "click." Some people are just hard to get to know, maybe even difficult. If we want to be successful and keep a difficult customer's business, we must find a way to make it work. We don't ask customers to change their point of view or what they expect from us; we figure it out – we find a solution! We do everything we can think of to build a relationship with customers to make sure they are happy. We provide Cherry on Top service, doing unexpected and special things to give the customer the best possible experience with us and our company.

This is how you should think of your relationship with your boss. You should always approach your relationship with your boss as if he/she were your best customer. That's what Cliff finally understood: to be successful, he had to provide extra value. If he wanted to change his schedule, he had to improve so he could be on his boss' agenda. And it was up to Cliff to figure out a way to get there.

From time to time, I would check in with Cliff to see how things were going at work. During one conversation, Cliff was complaining (again) about his boss. Finally, I said, "Cliff, be happy or be gone." It's as simple as that. If you're not happy, and you're not willing to change your attitude, work habits, or opinions, then you need to leave the organization and move on. Sometimes people aren't a good fit for the company or their bosses, and that's okay. The sooner everyone realizes that, the better for all. I truly believe this.

Be happy or be gone.

So, how do you manage your relationship with your boss? The word that comes to mind is to be "proactive." For example, don't wait for the question(s); offer the answer before the question is even asked. Anticipate what he/she is going to require and have it ready. On days when my calendar was booked with back-to-back conference calls and meetings, I was always appreciative when my assistant appeared at my desk with a grilled chicken salad with balsamic vinaigrette. To me, that was a cherry on top. She showed unexpected care and thoughtfulness in anticipating my needs and helping to make my day a little easier. Figure out what your boss' hot buttons are and her preferred communication style: does she like to communicate face to face, or via email? Is he a morning person or a night owl? What are the top three things that you need to achieve this year to make an "A?"

Highly effective employees make it a point to keep their bosses informed and in the loop. If you don't have recurring meetings or regularly scheduled time to catch up and touch base, fix that immediately. Ask for time on his/her calendar. Your manager might not be aware of everything you are working on and all of your contributions. These meetings are a good time to highlight the progress you've made on projects or assignments, and/or ask for their help or opinion. If your boss doesn't check in with you, be proactive and check in with him or her.

At one time, I had 15 direct reports. That is a significant number of people to manage and keep up with. My colleague Sarah and I have worked together since January 1989, and over the years, I have often asked her to help me with a new project, or an "ASAP" item. When she is completely swamped with work and deadlines, Sarah says, "Joyce, I am happy to help you with that, however, I am also working on x, y, and z," and she provides me with the specifics. Sometimes, I have been unaware of all the things that Sarah had in the queue (her "to do" list). I truly appreciate it when she has outlined what she has going on and asked for my help in prioritizing her work. This approach is valuable to me because we always have a clear understanding of the priorities and the next steps. We are on the same page. Being completely aligned in expectations is what employees and managers want. We want to be in sync with each other. And, in a professional way, Sarah has managed her relationship with me by reprioritizing her work to align with her boss' agenda.

During my career, I've had many bosses and hundreds of direct reports. I've learned what makes a good employee and how to be a good employee. From both perspectives, here are some of those lessons (see Figure 2 on next page).

Learning how to "manage up" is just as important as "managing down." Cliff was a terrific manager of people; his team loved him, and they would "jump through hoops" for him. He was great at "managing down," specifically, his direct reports, but he didn't have a clue about "managing up," his boss, until we had that ongoing conversation.

I've had the privilege to work with many outstanding leaders. Some of these leaders were very good at "managing up" and had strong relationships with senior leaders and executives. However, when it came to the people on their own teams, the reviews were not as good. The very best leaders know how to put a cherry on top in all their relationships – with team members and their boss.

Figure 2 – Lessons on what makes a good employee and how to be a good employee

**Number one: Be positive and optimistic, no matter what.** Attitude always outshines aptitude. Period.

**Number two: Perform and achieve the results.** The numbers don't lie, and your results always speak for themselves.

**Number three: No surprises.** Surprises are fun for birthday parties, but not in business. If there is an issue, don't wait for your boss to hear the news thirdhand. Go straight "to the fire" and let him/her know about the problem immediately.

**Number four: Create solutions, not problems.** Be the person who comes to the table with solutions, not the person who blames and complains. See #1 above.

**Number five: Overcommunicate.** Always, always, always. Most problems are caused by miscommunication. Clear and consistent communication boosts productivity because everyone is informed and clear on the message(s).

**Number six: Stay relevant.** Disrupt yourself and learn. Read and stay up to date on current topics, trends, and technology. Admit when you don't know something; it's okay to be uncomfortable. Take time to learn, and never stop growing.

**Number seven: Be low maintenance.** In *When Harry Met Sally*, Harry (Billy Crystal) tells Sally (Meg Ryan), while they are each separately watching *Casablanca* and talking on the phone, that Ingrid Bergman is "low maintenance." He says there are two types of women: high maintenance and low maintenance. Sally asks, "Which one am I?" And Harry responds, "You're the worst kind. You're high maintenance, but you think you're low maintenance."
High-maintenance people are generally needy and require a lot of time and attention. They are difficult, inflexible, and picky (like Sally with her salad dressing on the side). Low-maintenance people manage themselves; they know what to do, and they get the job done without somebody holding their hand. They are independent "go-getters."

Number eight: **No drama.** Have you ever noticed there are people in your life who constantly have drama going on? It is exhausting to work with someone who is always in the middle of a crisis, either at work or at home. As I like to say, be a "No-Drama Mama." No-Drama Mamas are so much easier to work with and fun to be around.

Number nine: **Focus on the customer.** We have many customers including our boss, our employees, our clients, our family members, our friends – anyone we interact with at work or in our personal life. As my friend Bess Davis likes to say, "Be interested and interesting." Connect with people on a personal level, and listen more than you talk.

Number ten: **Know the animal you're tracking.** The more you know about someone – their habits, likes and dislikes, strengths and weaknesses, what brings them joy, what they value, what motivates them – the more effectively you will be able to work together and have a strong relationship. As Sir Francis Bacon said, "Knowledge is power."

# Cherry on Top #9: Outwork the Competition

I have always loved to work and outwork the competition. From the time I claimed the tomato fields and set up my stand, work has been a big part of my life. I am blessed to have a super high energy level, and one thing I have always known for certain: I can outwork the competition.

Mary Cady Webb opened a small children's shop in 1947 that she expanded into Pompano Beach, Florida's first ladies' ready-to-wear store, Mary Webb's. She grew the business to include a complete ladies' department store, a bridal shop, gift shop, and two additional specialty stores located in Boca Raton.

Mary was a friend of my parents, and one evening, they were attending a social function together. During the course of the conversation, Mary asked my mother if one of the Collier girls would want to work at her Oceanside store during inventory. When I was in high school, the thought of making money working at "Miss Mary's" sounded wonderful to me, and I immediately jumped at the opportunity.

The following holiday season, Miss Mary asked me to work in the gift-wrapping area, and from there, I moved to selling on the floor, and then managing the bridal department. I quickly developed the knack for selling wedding dresses. Mary Webb's bridal department was perfectly appointed (for the late '70s) with a white shag carpet, mirrored walls, and a round elevated platform that the bride-to-be stood on when trying on potential dresses. It was a princess-like experience! I had an eye for knowing which style dress would be most flattering on the bride. I would help clients by selecting dresses that would complement their body type and accentuate their best assets. Mary Webb paid a bonus for every wedding dress that was sold. I quickly learned that this meant that for every dress I sold, I would earn extra money. This is my first memory of being on an incentive plan, and I loved it!

When I was in college, I continued working at Mary Webb's during the summers. I asked to be on the schedule as many days as I could because I knew the more hours I worked, the more dresses I would sell, and the more money I would make. One of the benefits of working at Mary Webb's was that I could buy clothes at a discount and put them on my store account. When I got paid, Miss Mary applied my paycheck to my account. This was a big motivator for a college student who wanted new clothes and shoes for going back to school in the fall! In all the time I worked there, I don't ever remember bringing home a paycheck, but I always had new clothes!

A high energy level and a strong work ethic are half of what it takes to beat the competition. The other half is having the discipline, the will, and the competitive fire that drives you to work harder and to be better than everyone else. We see this in professional athletes: a fierce, competitive will to win and the desire and willingness to work extra hard to achieve personal goals. Tiger Woods' 2019 Masters win is an example of drive, perseverance, and outworking the competition. The amount of time and work Tiger devoted to regaining his form to be able to compete and win at the highest level after physical and personal setbacks is unfathomable. It's more than putting in the workouts; it's having the inner grit to compete against the best in the world and win.

"Enthusiasm is common.
Endurance is rare."
— Angela Duckworth

At Adecco, we witness firsthand this same discipline and work ethic in the Olympic and Paralympic athletes we work with through our partnership with the United States Olympic and Paralympic Committee and the Athlete Career and Education program. Savannah Graybill is a member of Team USA and the Women's Skeleton National Team. Savannah is working with the Adecco Group's communication team while she is training for the 2022 Winter Olympic Games in Beijing, China.

For a skeleton athlete, on-ice training and competition take place from October through the beginning of April. During this time, Savannah is devoting 30-40 hours per week to a rigorous schedule that includes sprinting, weight lifting, sliding, mental preparation, and sled preparation. In the offseason, she continues her training regime by sprinting, weight lifting, push training, phone calls with coaches and trainers, and mental preparation – "mind runs" in which she visualizes sliding the track.

For 11 months of the year, Savannah is training six days a

week. Sundays are her days off, and she takes a break during the month of April to recharge, refocus, and spend quality time with her family in Pennsylvania.

Savannah's Olympic journey began in 2011, and in 2018, she was an alternate for the PyeongChang 2018 Olympic Winter Games. Team trials take place in October, and every year Savannah has to earn the right to be a member of the team. The goal in the off-Olympic years is to make the World Cup team and compete in the World Championships.

"At the end of the day, you have to earn it, and that has to come from inside," Savannah says. "You match your training to your competitor's training, but you have to have that extra little piece inside of you. Each small step now builds to the 'wow' factor later. You have to have that one small thing intrinsically. You can choose to put in the work or choose to put in half the work – that part comes from within you."

**Nothing takes the place
of hard work.**

Top-performing salespeople understand that sales is not a part-time job. Like Savannah and other top athletes, you must be committed, driven, and disciplined. You have to have a plan and work the plan. From my experience, I've learned that some people like to talk about their plans and hard work, and others are real workers and actually get the job done. There are lots of "talkers," but I like the "doers," the people who work hard and drive the business forward by getting the strategic priorities ("the big rocks") accomplished.

People often think there is a "magic bullet" for success, but I have yet to find a shortcut for hard work. During a visit to a large Northeast market, I was having lunch at a casual Asian restaurant with the branch manager of our downtown office. There is tons of business in large metropolitan markets for staffing companies, and Nick's branch was underperforming. The office was marginally profitable, and I knew we could do more in the market. I suspected that Nick wasn't making sales calls and working up to his potential.

Right after we sat down at the restaurant, Nick asked me in a somewhat solicitous, charming manner, "Joyce, you've been so successful in the industry – how have you done that?" I was so taken aback by Nick's question that I responded by reaching under the table and taking off the shoe on my left foot and holding it in my right hand with the bottom of the shoe facing Nick on the other side of the table. I said, "Nick, you know that you're very professional, well trained, smart, and prepared. If you take that and a little shoe leather out on the street and make calls, you'll get orders." I let Nick know that I knew that he wasn't making the calls and doing the work.

When people tell me that they're making sales calls, but we don't see the results, one of two things is happening: either they can't sell, because they're making the calls but nobody's buying, or, they aren't selling and making the calls.

For Nick, he wasn't selling. Nothing takes the place of face-to-face sales and the opportunity to build a relationship with a client.

My favorite story that perfectly illustrates this idea is one I originally heard from Ray Roe, called "Five Frogs on a Log." It goes like this. There are five frogs on a log, and one decides to jump in the pond. How many frogs are left on the log? The answer is "five," because deciding and doing are two different things. The workers, the doers, are the people who act. They do more than talk; they decide to do something, and then they jump off the log and get to work! The talkers are "all hat and no cattle." Talkers talk a good game, but when it comes to actual work and results, they often disappoint.

John Foley, a former lead solo pilot of the Blue Angels, was the keynote speaker at Adecco's 2015 Leadership Summit. It is awe-inspiring to hear him speak about flying a high-performance, 18-ton aircraft at speeds up to 700 mph just one arm's length away from the wingtip of a teammate's jet. John knows about commitment, preparation, and what it takes to perform at the highest level. When he told our group, "Some people want it to happen. Some people wish it would happen. Others make it happen," this resonated with me and has strongly influenced me to this day.

When I speak at conferences and on panels, I am often asked how I became the president of one of the largest staffing companies in the United States. I always answer this question the same way: "The harder I worked, the luckier I got." There's no magic bullet for success; it boils down to being willing to work hard and do the things that others can't or don't want to do. It's about taking action: doing rather than deciding (like the five frogs on a log), having a sense of urgency about what you are trying to accomplish, and making personal sacrifices.

When you take on a big role, a few extra things come with your new title: more is expected of you, the responsibility and the problems are bigger, and your time is not your own. You have to be "all in," and that means your life revolves around the business, not the other way around. There were many, many nights when I would be sitting in my driveway on the phone in my car finishing a call while David and the boys would be waiting for me to have dinner. After 20 minutes or so, David would come out of the house and put his hands in the air as if to ask, "Are you joining us?" I would wrap up the call as quickly as I could and run into the house explaining to him, "David, I get paid to be inconvenienced." Thank goodness David was understanding and supportive. Having worked in management for a large global company, David knew that unexpected issues often arise late in the day, and I had to be available.

Today, many women in senior leadership roles are expected to travel almost every week and work long hours. I know many of my friends and colleagues have struggled with the desire to be at home with their husbands and children while also wanting the big job. It's tough, and I understand that. I also know that it's very difficult to "have it all." Our children's lives are full of things we want to be a part of: school plays, parent-teacher conferences, doctor and orthodontist appointments, awards ceremonies, dance recitals, basketball games, and many milestones including getting a driver's license, going to the prom, and visiting college campuses. As a working mom in a senior role, it's not possible to be home and to be a part of everything. You have to have a great support system, which I was grateful to have with David, and you have to make the hard choices.

In 2009, I had the good fortune to meet Suzy Welch during an Adecco Group breakfast book series that we held for clients across America. Suzy is smart, warm, has a witty sense of humor, and is the author of one of my favorite books, *10-10-10: A Life-Transforming Idea*. I was completely mesmerized while Suzy spoke about "10-10-10" and how she developed this idea as a life management tool when faced with tough decisions.

It took me a long time to figure this out – when you're just starting out in your career, you're so eager to learn as much as you can and advance quickly, that sometimes you forget to take care of yourself or the other aspects of your life outside of work. The advice I would give to my younger self is to remember that your work and home life is like a seesaw: sometimes it's more weighted toward work, and other times tilted more toward home and family. Rather than thinking of it as two distinct universes, I prefer to look at it as my one life, and I manage it the best I can.

Welch's "10-10-10" rule has been life-changing for me. The rule makes you ask yourself, "What will this decision mean to me in 10 minutes, 10 months, 10 years?" It puts every scenario into perspective, and allows you to make practical and confident decisions.

When the boys were in high school, David's travel schedule was more flexible and less hectic than mine, and he was able to attend all of Coleman's lacrosse games. Before Coleman's senior season started, he said, "Mom, could you please try to make it to every home game?" This was important to Coleman, and I promised him that I would see him play in every home lacrosse game his senior year before graduating from high school.

That year, a devastating tsunami hit Japan, and the economic impact was felt around the world, including in the United States, as manufacturers struggled with getting parts and products from Asia. When manufacturers don't have the parts to build their products, lines start to shut down, and employees are at risk for layoffs. Stopped production costs can be enormous, possibly exceeding one million dollars per hour in downtime expense. One of our largest customers, an automotive company, called an emergency meeting to talk about the impact the tsunami was having on their production and how Adecco's support was needed during this time. They specifically asked that I attend the meeting to participate in the strategy session about production and staffing levels while they weathered the storm.

I would have been very happy to attend the meeting, but as luck would have it, the meeting was on the same day as Coleman's last home lacrosse match. As a working mother, I was completely torn between the desire to support my son and my obligations as an executive to the company and to the customer. I experienced an intellectual and emotional battle as I struggled with what to do, and how to make the decision. It was logistically impossible to attend the meeting and be at Coleman's game. The problem was that I wanted to do both, and I didn't want to disappoint either. The truth of the matter is that I didn't know what to do. I felt pulled by two important and conflicting priorities.

As I tried to find a way to help the client and not disappoint my son during his final year of high school, my stress level was "off the charts." Being at Coleman's match was the only thing he had asked of me, yet I felt pulled by my professional responsibilities as the president of the company. Then I remembered Suzy Welch's book talk, and I asked myself: "What will be the impact of this decision in 10 minutes, 10 months, and 10 years?" It was only then that I began to have clarity about what to do.

In 10 minutes, the customer would be disappointed to learn that I would not be able to attend the meeting. But, I had a strong team, and I had complete confidence in the colleague who would attend in my place. I knew she was fully capable of representing Adecco and working with the customer on solutions. In 10 months, the customer would not even remember that I was not at the meeting. If I attended the meeting, in 10 months my relationship with Coleman would be strained since I had not kept my promise to him. When he would learn that I had chosen to attend the meeting, he would likely respond, "That's okay, Mom, you always choose work." And in 10 years, my company would still have that strong customer relationship. But at Coleman's rehearsal dinner the night before his wedding, the crack that had formed between us that spring during lacrosse season might have become a chasm that couldn't be crossed.

It's a challenge for women in leadership roles to find the right balance between work and home life and to juggle business and personal priorities. I am grateful to Suzy Welch for her wisdom and simple formula for making tough decisions that often have complicated repercussions.

Another opportunity for balance is planning vacation time. For most of my career, I believed I had to check emails, be on conference calls, and tend to other work-related things while I was on vacation. This is what was expected, and what I thought was "normal" – and others followed suit.

PTO – what should stand for Personal Time Off – started being called Pretend Time Off. I would often return from a week of PTO feeling like I had never left the office. I was still plugged-in and "on the grid" the entire time. In retrospect, I was not a very good role model when it came to the whole "work/life balance" thing.

Ten years into my career, a friend mentioned The Ashram Spa Resort in Calabasas, California, to me. She described the retreat as a weeklong intensive "getaway" from the hustle and bustle of daily and career life. No cell phones, computers, or any sort of technology would be permitted, although the chance of boredom was slim to none. The Ashram planned various activities every day that guests were required to participate in, from yoga to cooking, allowing participants the chance not only to leave work at the door, but also to "rejuvenate" themselves.

I'd be lying if I said the idea didn't sound nice, but at the time, it also sounded unfathomable. With a full-time career, two sons, and a slew of constant travel to juggle, I stored the idea away for a later time. That time came in 2018 when, during the second week of October, I found myself unpacking my suitcase at The Ashram. While the idea had sounded nice 20 years prior, and perhaps even at the time I booked my stay, I suddenly found myself out of my comfort zone. Without my cell phone, along with the other daily staples I'd been stripped of (including caffeine and sugar), I couldn't help but question what I'd signed myself up for. I really didn't know whether I'd be able to leave work at the door.

For the next seven days, I woke up at 5:30 every morning, went to yoga at 6:00, and breakfast at 7:00, and then spent the following 30-minute increments of every day participating in various "transformative" activities. I hiked over 10 miles. I watched the sunrise every morning. I exercised muscles in my body I had forgotten existed. I ate clean foods that fueled me for the multiple physical activities I participated in daily. Halfway through my stay at The Ashram, something started to happen.

Without the option to check my emails, I put my energy toward checking what activity was next on the daily schedule. By not being involved in issues at work, I put my focus on trusting my colleagues to handle any crisis that might arise in my absence. I started thinking about myself instead, and leaning into the experience.

In a 2018 Gallup survey studying the US full-time workforce, 28% of millennials claimed they frequently experience burnout at work. An additional 45% of millennials said they sometimes feel burned out at work, totaling 73% of millennials experiencing some sort of burnout while on the clock – and that's just one segment of our workforce. Studies show employees who experience burnout are 63% more likely to take a sick day and are two- to three-times more likely to leave their current employer.

It took me 30 years, but in just one week, I learned a valuable lesson. After seven days of unplugging, I returned to my home in Charlotte and my career at Adecco, ready not only to embrace whatever was waiting for me, but excited to embrace it!

If we want to keep our high performers – and if we want our high performers to continue to perform – we must instill a Real Time Off vs. Pretend Time Off culture. Vacation time is not only earned, it should be used to truly disengage and give your mind, body, and spirit a break from what typically occupies your Monday – Friday 8am – 5pm, (or, if you are like me, your 24/7).

If you struggle to truly take and enjoy your PTO, here are four principles you need to remember. I learned these while at The Ashram:

- It's okay to disengage; give yourself permission
- Take time for yourself to re-energize and revitalize
- Focus on your health and well-being
- By taking the time to disengage we are more engaged at work

I'm not alone in my prior struggles to use my PTO. According to a Glassdoor and Harris Interactive survey reported by Forbes, only 25% of Americans use all of their paid vacation days. A paper published in the *Journal of Happiness Studies* evaluating the importance of paid time off found people felt less tense and healthier after returning from a vacation, with higher energy levels and more life satisfaction overall.

Whether an employer or employee, taking time off from work should be a staple in your company's corporate culture. I am an apostle of PTO being RTO.

My friend Gay Gaddis is an example of work-life integration and true grit. In 1989, Gay started her company, T3—The Think Tank, after cashing in a $16,000 IRA. Today, T3 has offices nationwide and creates innovative digital marketing programs for Fortune 200 clients. T3 is a top-ranked innovation firm, one of the largest advertising agencies owned by a woman.

A few years after Gay launched her company, four key members of her team became pregnant, and Gay faced a mini-crisis in her business. Gay would be challenged to continue to provide high-quality marketing services to her clients while her staff members were out on maternity leave, or chose to opt out of the workplace altogether. As a mother herself, Gay understood and was sympathetic to the new mothers on her team, so she came up with a creative solution for all. She announced a groundbreaking policy that allowed new mothers to bring their babies to work until they started to crawl and /or walk.

Gay was gritty enough to start her own business, resilient enough to navigate the tough times, and smart enough to give birth to a new work-life balance benefit for her employees.

Angela Duckworth argues in her book, *Grit: The Power of Passion and Perseverance*, that grit matters more than talent, and I would agree. She writes, "I won't just have a job; I'll have a calling. I'll challenge myself every day. When I get knocked down, I'll get back up. I may not be the smartest person in the room, but I'll strive to be the grittiest."

Whether you call it resilience, perseverance, or grit,

having the inner strength to push forward even when it's hard is one of the most important traits of high-performing employees and leaders. When Hillary Clinton conceded the race for the presidency in 2008, she told her supporters, "Although we weren't able to shatter that highest, hardest glass ceiling this time, thanks to you, it's got about 18 million cracks in it and the light is shining through like never before, filling us all with the hope and the sure knowledge that the path will be a little easier next time."

When I speak on panels and attend conferences, I am often asked what I think about "the glass ceiling." My answer is simple: "I never saw a glass ceiling because I was too busy working with my head down, and I never looked up." My advice is to outwork the competition, deliver the results, be positive, dare to be different, always add value, and raise your hand and keep it raised.

# Cherry on Top #10:  Pay Attention to Detail

Putting a cherry on top means that you take time and put thought into what you do. As we said earlier, the cherry on top is about thoughtfulness and care. When you pay attention to detail, you are essentially telling someone, "I care enough about this and you to make sure I get it right." Imagine, for a moment these scenarios:

- Receiving a box of chocolates that contain nuts from your husband, partner, friend, or whomever, and you have a peanut allergy.
- Getting a birthday or anniversary card from a senior manager at work addressed to "Elizabeth," when you go by "Betsy."
- Receiving a bottle of wine, and you don't drink alcohol.

How would that make you feel? Probably pretty disappointed, as you silently think to yourself, "This person doesn't even know me." Some might say, "Well, it's no big deal, it's the thought that matters." And I would say that *it is the thought and attention to detail that express the care and love that matter*.

There are no perfect people – we talked about this in Chapter Six. No one wakes up to mess up. Occasionally, mistakes happen, but I believe that by taking the extra time, thought, and care to pay attention to detail, we can minimize mistakes – and put more cherries on top. Every so often, a huge mistake is made that is almost unimaginable, and most often it's due to not paying attention to detail.

On one occasion, a colleague left her new laptop in her unlocked car in a shopping mall parking lot. Upon hearing this news, I was speechless because it was incredible to me that someone could make such a ridiculous and costly mistake. But once I had a moment to think about what had occurred, I realized that in that mall parking lot, Sophia had experienced what I call, "Temporary Insanity." Temporary Insanity can happen to anyone, including me. At work and at home, there have been instances of Temporary Insanity, and I've made it my policy to forgive Temporary Insanity one time. I chalk it up to forgetfulness, lack of focus, or just carelessness. When a mistake like this occurs, I have a conversation with the person and gently explain that I am willing to forgive Temporary Insanity one time, but if something of this magnitude occurs in the future, we'll be having a different conversation. Forgiving someone for Temporary Insanity is a large deposit in the Emotional Bank Account, especially if the employee thinks they're going to be terminated. I prefer to have an "attitude of latitude." Giving someone a second chance helps to build your relationship with them, and it shows that you have someone's back, even in the tough times. When you look for the good in everyone and everything, even when it's difficult, you are living and leading with an "abundance" mentality. This is powerfully influential.

In my office hangs a gold-framed 30- x 36-inch portrait of William Bayard, Jr. The painting doesn't fit with the rest of the office decor, but I keep it hanging right in front of my desk to remind me of one thing: the importance of attention to detail.

William Bayard portrait
on the wall in my office

On a Saturday night in 2015, I received an urgent phone call from one of our colleagues who was attending a charity event in New York City with her husband. Tammy was excited because one of the items in the silent auction was an original portrait of one of the founders of Bank of America. Bank of America World Headquarters is about two blocks from my office in downtown Charlotte, and I have a clear view of its 60-story building from my office window. One of my friends is on the leadership team of the bank, and Tammy and I talked about how we could purchase the painting in the silent auction and then donate it to the bank for their history collection/archives.

Tammy was so excited about the painting, its history, and my connection to the bank that I gave her the "green light" to bid on the painting. The next morning, Tammy texted me to report she won the portrait in the silent auction for $1,600. We arranged for her to have it carefully packed, crated, and shipped to my office so I could present it to Bank of America for their collection.

A couple of weeks later, a huge box arrived at the office via UPS, and we couldn't wait to unpack it. It took three of us 10 minutes to remove the painting from the crate and wrapping. Finally, the image was revealed: a distinguished gentleman with white hair and attractive features dressed in clothing traditional in George Washington's era: a white ruffled shirt and black button jacket. On the reverse side of the painting, we found these words:

*This copy was painted*
*by Wallace Bryant in 1920*
*from the original portrait by*
*Frederick* (last name indistinguishable).
*The portrait is that of*
*William Bayard*
*Second President of The Bank of America*
*1814-1816*

Upon doing a little internet research, we learned that William Bayard, Jr. was born in New York City in 1761. He was a prominent banker and businessman and a close friend of Alexander Hamilton. "The Bank of America" noted on the back of the painting was one of the first financial institutions in the United States, founded by Alexander Hamilton but unrelated to the modern financial services corporation, Bank of America, whose name and roots date back to 1904 in California.

Rather than being known as a founding father of today's Bank of America, William Bayard is known for being instrumental in the creation of the Erie Canal. And, it was in William Bayard's home that Alexander Hamilton died the day after he was shot by Aaron Burr. In our exuberance, we had spent a lot of money for a copy of an original painting of a man who has a place in America's history – but not with Bank of America.

**Details matter. It's worth waiting to get it right.**
— Steve Jobs

William Bayard's portrait in my office is a constant reminder of the importance of attention to detail. As a "big picture" extrovert, I am the first to admit that I can easily get caught up in the excitement of what's happening, and often don't slow down long enough to pay attention to the details.

Overlooking details and rushing to get things done can have more serious consequences than buying the wrong portrait reproduction at a charity silent auctio When I was president of Adecco's business line, one my ongoing responsibilities was to review the qua incentive payments for colleagues. This involved st more than 20 large Excel files containing calcula hundreds of colleagues. In my role, one of th was always passionate about was that our bonuses were correct and paid on time. I had a fiduciary responsibility to the company to ensure that the incentive files had been properly scrubbed, scrutinized, and studied before they were sent to Colleague Payroll for payment. Three other levels in the organization had reviewed the files before they were sent to my office for final approval.

It would be very easy to open each worksheet, do a cursory review, and think, "That looks about right," and approve the files. Fortunately, my colleague Sarah is highly conscientious. She carved out time in her schedule to review every incentive file in detail, and when she spotted something that "didn't add up," she raised a question or asked for additional review or explanation. Because she is so meticulous and I care so much about making sure that people are compensated correctly, over the years Sarah (also known as "Eagle Eye") and I found thousands of dollars in errors – either overpayments or underpayments.

Another instance of the importance of attention to detail is in the RFP process. In the staffing industry, customers ᵗt their business out to bid, and companies have the ᵗunity to respond to a Request for Proposal ("RFP"), a ᵔument in which you outline the benefits, services, ᵗ ᵉ of working with your company. After the ᵛwed all of the submitted proposals, the ᵗ three to five) are invited to make ᵗn committee.

ᵗs when we truly have the ᵗselves from our competitors. ᵗs will bring in their "A Teams" ᵗding flying in executives and senior management from around the country. Very sharp PowerPoint presentations are prepared in nice binders, and everyone wears their best dresses and suits. For some people, these presentations can make or break a career. The final presentations often take place in boardrooms with the PowerPoint slides shot up on a screen while the staffing company representatives take turns presenting, explaining why their company should be selected as the number one supplier of temp staffing services, and be awarded the multi-million-dollar contract.

Our RFP presentation to a major company that specializes in personalized printing products stands out as a stellar example of attention to detail. In South Carolina, the company has a large location there where they produce their cards and photo books. It is a wonderful company to work for, a "love brand," and a company that Adecco has wanted in our client portfolio for a very long time. Adecco had a small amount of business with the company, and I had several relationships with members of their team. When their business came up for bid, we were fortunate to be invited to the presentation stage. The bid included their locations in South Carolina, Minnesota, and Arizona, and we absolutely wanted to win the business!

Our sales team did a tremendous amount of work preparing for the presentation. We strategized about the best way to present Adecco's value-driven solutions to the selection committee in a clear, professional, compelling way. We brainstormed how we could put a cherry on top of our presentation and truly distinguish ourselves from our competitors. On the day of the meeting, rather than review all of our information in a PowerPoint deck, the Adecco team presented each member of the committee with a personalized book like one produced by the client, which contained our presentation and our clearly defined value proposition. We took the time, thought, care, and effort to customize the sales presentation and to pay attention to the details. We put a cherry on top, and we won the business.

Early in my career, we established a relationship with one of the leading banks in the country based in Charlotte, and they were a highly valued client for many years. During this time, staffing became more and more sophisticated, as companies realized the benefits of supplemental staffing, so the dollars being spent on staffing continued to rise. Large companies began to centralize their staffing spend as a way to manage and gain control of all of the vendors and expenses. At the same time, the purchasing decision shifted from the Personnel Department (now known as "Human Resources") to Purchasing.

When I heard the news that the bank had hired a new senior vice president and that she planned to put the staffing business out for Request for Proposal ("RFP"), I was extremely worried that we could be at risk for losing the business. The bank was working with more than 50 vendors, Adecco being one of them, and I had learned that the CEO was close personal friends with someone at one of our large international competitors. Although we had done a good job of working with the bank, we were in "The Danger Zone," big time.

The bank's new SVP wanted to send the RFP to the

"big players" in the staffing space. As is common with procurement people, she was extremely skeptical about salespeople and their promises. She and her team were tasked with selecting the highest-quality staffing companies to support the bank, and to realize cost savings in consolidating their purchasing from 50+ vendors to three. I knew we had a huge challenge ahead of us, and we would have to earn the right to retain the business.

After a thorough review of all of the pages and pages of proposals submitted, the bank invited the top finalists to present their service offering on-site before the selection committee in Charlotte. The senior vice president (and self-proclaimed cynic) described our presentation as follows:

"On the day of the presentation in Charlotte, Joyce arrived with other executives from the Adecco Group. This was important because the committee was able to meet and hear from senior leaders of Adecco, Modis, Accounting Principals and Lee Hecht Harrison – all Adecco Group companies who would be supporting the bank under a new contract.

"After introducing the colleagues who had traveled to Charlotte to attend the meeting with her, Joyce began the presentation by taking out her checkbook, holding it open, and saying, 'I am a customer of the bank, and Charlotte is my hometown.' She then covered her part of the presentation with an overview of the Adecco Group, the history of their relationship with the bank, and she outlined Adecco's value proposition.

"The Adecco Group executive who followed Joyce began by saying, 'You are my bank,' and he placed his credit cards on the conference room table. And this continued with the third executive, who started his section of the presentation with, 'I've chosen you as my bank – including my home mortgage and car loans.'

"During their presentation, each Adecco Group business leader explained how the bank was important to them personally, and they expressed pride and trust in us as their financial services provider. Adecco brought their high-level leadership in, and they personalized the sales presentation. This was a huge differentiator for us, and it made Adecco stand out from the other staffing companies we were considering. Many companies bring in the big shots, but they don't personalize the presentation."

Attention to detail is important because not only can it help you win new business; investing time up front can save significant time and money – and prevent problems in the future. There are just certain things for which it doesn't pay to cut corners: offer letters, incentive plans, hotel contracts, client contracts, pricing worksheets, and legal agreements of every variety. Unfortunately, many people would rather "check the box" than take the time to complete the necessary (and sometimes tedious) due diligence. It takes focus, patience, and your undivided attention to make sure that everything is as it should be.

I've had the privilege of working with Dr. George Watts, a behavioral scientist with a doctorate in counseling psychology from the College of William and Mary. Dr. Watts espouses the value of conscientiousness: "The personality trait of conscientiousness adds strategic value because the mindset drives both the top and bottom line.

It's about superior outcomes built on a commitment to thoroughness. Ultimately, conscientiousness breaks complexity into processes that deliver excellence. It is a real differentiator and ultimately why both people and companies win."

I have found that highly conscientious people are driven to do things right, and they take time to pay attention to the details. They "want" to do a good job, rather than "try" to do a good job.

Attention to detail is important in everything we do. It's how we put a cherry on top of colleague and client events. When I'm planning an event, I take a moment to think, "What would make this better – what would be a cherry on top for our colleagues or clients?" This type of thinking carries over into my personal life. For example, when I am selecting a gift for someone or planning a dinner, I make an extra effort to prepare my guests' favorite dish, or to personalize a gift, such as hand towels, with a monogram.

Attention to detail means that you feel the card stock quality, you check every line of a report, you personalize your presentations, and you don't settle for less. You make the investments and make the time to do more.

# Cherry on Top #11: Never Let Anyone or Anything Change Who You Are

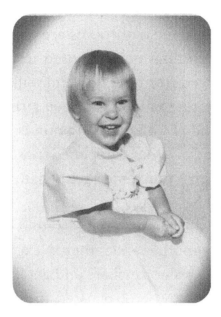

My baby picture at age 3.

As a child, I was cheerful, polite, and outgoing, a "happy-go-lucky" child eager to please my parents and teachers, with many friends in the neighborhood and at school. I was very fortunate to have what some would consider an idyllic childhood. My mom and dad were members of First United Methodist Church in Pompano Beach. First Methodist was five blocks from our house. At exactly 9:30 a.m., Dad would announce, "Girls, we are leaving for church in 10 minutes, and if you're not in the car, you'll be walking." I guess that was God's way of putting me on a diet and getting me to exercise because several Sunday mornings, I walked to church. After Sunday school and the service, Karyn, Kristi, and I would return from church wearing our pretty dresses to help our mother prepare Sunday lunch. I always tried to do the right thing. I was the type of child who sat in the front row of class and was an "eraser clapper" – the teacher's pet.

One day when I was in junior high school ("middle school"), I ran into the girl's bathroom during lunch. As is true at many schools, the bathrooms are hangouts for kids who are more often than not supposed to be somewhere else. When I emerged from the stall and walked toward the sink, I was quickly surrounded by three girls who were all bigger than me, and at 5'4" and 100 pounds, that was most of the student body. What happened next, I will never forget: one of the girls called me a nasty name and violently smashed a ripe mango on my forehead.

That night at the dinner table, I retold the bathroom mango story to my mother and father. Next, I explained all the ways that I planned to retaliate and get back at the girls who had humiliated and embarrassed me at school. After listening to my story and payback plans, my father very gently said, "Joyce, never let anyone or anything change who you are." At that moment, my hopes of retribution were dashed. Of course, Dad was right – if I were to do something ugly and hurtful, I'd be just like the girls in the bathroom, and that wasn't who I was as a human being.

I decided in that moment to always be me, just Joyce. This is the name I had given myself at age 6. My mother and father had named me Kimberly Joyce Collier – that's the name on my birth certificate and my college degree from Baylor. My middle name, Joyce, is in honor of my father's sister, Joyce Covington. At times, I was called "Kimberly Joyce," usually when I was being a little bit naughty. I became a decision-maker when I was 6 years old and told my mother, "My name is Joyce, not Kim."

Abraham Maslow, the 20th-century psychologist, is known for his concept of a "hierarchy of needs," his theory about what motivates human behavior. "Love/Belonging" is the third need in Maslow's pyramid of five basic needs. People want to be accepted and loved for who they are, and want to be part of a family, club, social group, or team. Sometimes, people will change to fit in and to be accepted because they want to belong.

To be authentic means to be genuine and real – not fake, not somebody who pretends to be someone else. Inauthentic or fake people put on a façade to be liked, accepted, popular, or simply, to "belong." In short, to be authentic means to be yourself in every situation and in all of your interactions. At Adecco, I was fortunate that I could be myself each and every day.

Amy Cuddy, a Princeton-trained social psychologist, became known for her 54 million-plus views of her 2012 TED Talk about body language and power posing. In December 2015, Amy published her first book, *Presence*, and two months later she spoke at Adecco's Leadership Summit in Orlando, Florida. In her book she writes, "By finding, believing, expressing, and then engaging our authentic best selves, especially if we do it right before our biggest challenges, we reduce our anxiety about social rejection and increase our openness to others. That allows us to be fully present."

In recent years, there has been a movement toward authenticity, with people wanting and expecting authenticity in all aspects of their lives, including their food, consumer products, social media, sports heroes, and political leaders. But most of all, we want authenticity in our relationships, including those with whom we work. We are our "authentic best selves," as Amy Cuddy describes, when we open ourselves up and allow others to see us as the unique and special individuals that we are. Authentic leaders are relatable, reliable, transparent, and thoughtful. They share the best of themselves with others and put a cherry on top.

"Three things in human life are important: the first is to be kind; the second is to be kind; and the third is to be kind."
— Henry James

When we're authentic, our words and actions align with our values. What we say and do is in harmony with our character and beliefs. Part of authenticity is having the personal courage, "the guts" to stand up for what you believe in, even if it's unpopular or could be personally detrimental. Not everybody has personal courage. Some people simply lack intestinal fortitude. But I've learned that sometimes you have to take risks. Julius Caesar speaks about courage in Shakespeare's play, *Julius Caesar*, "Cowards die many times before their deaths; the valiant never taste of death but once." I admire people who have personal courage.

It is a commonly known fact in baseball and softball that the players with the least experience and skills play the right field position. The majority of batters are right-handed and naturally pull the ball to left field. Therefore, right fielders rarely see any action. The summer before my freshman year in high school, that's where Coach Handrahan placed me when I started playing softball in the Pompano Beach summer softball league. I didn't field many balls that were hit through the infield, or make a lot of catches. However, I became quite adept at picking weeds, a skill I still possess and practice.

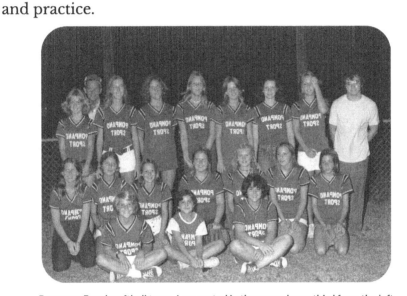

Pompano Beach softball team. I am seated in the second row, third from the left.

My softball career suddenly changed one day when the team's catcher was injured during a play at home plate and would be out for the rest of the season. Coach Handrahan called the team in and asked for a volunteer to play catcher. My hand shot straight up in the air as I said, "I'll play catcher!" By the end of the summer, I went from being the worst player on the team to being one of the best catchers in the city. I went from complete boredom and watching the grass grow in right field, to being in the middle of the action on every play behind the plate. I loved it, and I was good.

The following summer, my sister Kristi joined the team, and she was a worse player than I was when I started. During a critical part of a game with two outs and our team trailing in the score, Kristi struck out. I will never forget what happened next. Coach Handrahan rushed at Kristi, yelling and using horrible words that I had never heard an adult say before. He went on a tirade screaming at Kristi using the most awful language, with his face turning the color of a ripe tomato and his voice growing louder and louder. I ran over to where Coach Handrahan was standing on the field, and the team began to gather around. I said, "You cannot talk to my sister like that!" I was a good player, and I knew that Coach Handrahan needed me on the team playing catcher. I also knew in my heart that I couldn't play for a coach who would speak so ugly and hateful to my sister. To make my point to Coach Handrahan, I turned and walked off the field in the middle of the game.

Although I was a teenager at the time, and I had no leadership experience, this was an important moment for me that would help to form my leadership principles later in my life. As I reflect on what happened that summer day on the softball field, I learned that sometimes you have to "lay your body over" those you care about and stand up for what you believe is right.

While I was working with Ray Roe, we had a meeting in which we had to make a very difficult business decision that would financially impact one of my direct reports. There was a lot of debate back and forth, and virtually everyone around the conference table in Ray's office was arguing that this colleague should be held responsible for something that had been entirely out of his span of control. I disagreed with the argument that was being put forth. I was the only person in the entire room who defended our colleague, my direct report, and stood up for him. I had more insight into the issue than anyone else, so I felt an obligation to explain the entire situation and why he should not be penalized for something outside of his control.

I went out on a limb, and it was scary. When I got up the guts to express my point of view, the entire room went quiet, and everyone was staring at me. Finally, Ray spoke, "Joyce, you are right, and we are wrong. I have never been prouder of you than I am at this moment." That is when I learned about personal courage and having the guts to stand up for what you believe in. Shortly after that, I was promoted to chief operating officer. With Ray, I could go out on a limb and take risks, and I felt safe. Because Ray was always there to support me; he had me at the trunk.

As a young child, I was taught to mind my manners and be mindful of others, to know left from right and right from wrong, to pick up after myself, and to stand up for others. And since that day in junior high, I have tried to live by my father's advice and be myself: unequivocally and authentically Joyce.

# Cherry on Top #12:
# Make Your Last Job Your Best Job

Katharine Graham, the late publisher and CEO of *The Washington Post*, said, "To love what you do and feel that it matters, how could anything be more fun?" Throughout my career, this quote has resonated with me so much because it perfectly summarizes how I feel about my work and career with Adecco.

I am very lucky to have had the privilege of working with many wonderful and talented Cherry on Top people who are smart, passionate, fun, extremely hard-working, and committed to the mission of the company. For many years, Adecco Staffing's logo tagline was, "Better Work, Better Life." I always loved that because it succinctly expressed what we are all about and the core purpose of our work.

We work side by side with our clients and create staffing solutions that help their companies run efficiently and productively. Our associates fill important roles at many of the country's major employers. They help get new cars off the line, build navigation maps for the largest apps, and work in the medical equipment fields on products that save and improve American lives. They fill orders in warehouses and ensure that Christmas presents arrive on time, help manage America's power plants and supply energy to homes, and fill so many more important roles that improve the quality of life for everyone. I am quite sure that almost every American has used a product or service that Adecco associates have helped to build, support, or create.

I feel extremely grateful that my current role as president

of the Adecco Group US Foundation is the culmination of a lifetime of service in the staffing industry. Founded in 2019, the Foundation is committed to making the world of work a fairer, more accessible, and better place. Our vision is of a world where all people are enabled to reach their full potential. Our mission is to leverage the know-how and expertise of resources and groups to drive social value creation in the field of employment and skills.

We are not a grant-giving foundation, but rather a group of dedicated colleagues committed to accelerating new solutions in the world of work. We help people find their paths through programs that contribute to economic mobility, career progression, and work equality. Our focus is on making the future work for everyone.

I have always loved "The Starfish Story", adapted from *The Star Thrower*, a collection of poems and essays written by Loren Eisley (1907-1977) because it beautifully illustrates the difference that one person can make in the world with a simple act of kindness.

> *"Once upon a time, there was a wise man who used to go to the ocean to do his writing. He had a habit of walking on the beach before he began his work. One day, as he was walking along the shore, he looked down the beach and saw a human figure moving like a dancer. He smiled to himself at the thought of someone who would dance to the day, and so, he walked faster to catch up.*
>
> *As he got closer, he noticed that the figure was that of a young man, and that what he was doing was not dancing at all.*

*The young man was reaching down to the shore, picking up small objects, and throwing them into the ocean. He came closer still and called out, "Good morning! May I ask you what it is that you are doing?" The young man paused, looked up, and replied, "Throwing starfish into the ocean."*

*"I must ask, then, why are you throwing starfish into the ocean?" asked the somewhat startled wise man. To this, the young man replied, "The sun is up and the tide is going out. If I don't throw them in, they'll die." Upon hearing this, the wise man commented, "But, young man, do you not realize that there are many many miles of beach and there are starfish along every mile? You can't possibly make a difference."*

*At this, the young man bent down, picked up yet another starfish, and threw it into the ocean. As it met the water, he said, "It made a difference for that one."*

Even though we live in a big world with billions of people, each of us has the capacity to be a "Star Thrower." When we launched the Adecco Group US Foundation, our goal was to select one national charity to partner with that has a worthy purpose, does great work, and is in line with the mission of the Foundation. Like the young man in the starfish story, we also wanted to make an immediate impact.

For many years, I have been aware of the work that Dress for Success® does in Charlotte, and I have tremendous admiration for the executive director, Kerry Barr O'Connor, and the work she and her team do. Partnering with community leaders, leveraging resources, and working with other nonprofits, they provide much-needed services for Dress for Success clients.

Kerry has an incredible passion for her work. She says, "When you lift a woman out of poverty, as many as six family members will follow." Wow! Kerry Barr O'Connor and all of the Dress for Success colleagues and volunteers around the world are most certainly "Star Throwers."

The mission of Dress for Success is "to empower women to achieve economic independence by providing a network of support, professional attire, and the development tools to help women thrive in work and in life." Dress for Success has 150 locations in 25 countries.

This excellent organization helps women not only by providing professional clothing for work, but also by supporting its clients with job readiness training, including resume writing and interview skills, and other assistance and resources. Dress for Success was a perfect fit for us because of the synergies created by our shared missions.

In addition to organizing clothing drives ("the dress"), we are also focused on "success" by preparing women to enter or reenter the workforce. As an example, the Adecco Group colleagues in Atlanta hosted a workshop at Dress for Success for its clients with the theme "Success for Entering the Workforce." The workshop sessions included Cover Letters that Get Results, Resume Writing, Interview Tips & Tricks, a Q&A, and individual breakout sessions.

A Dress for Success client named Jennifer who attended the workshop had had a previous interview experience that left her feeling discouraged about her job search. A week after the workshop, the Adecco team received the following note from Dress for Success' programs and outreach coordinator:

*The ladies loved having you and learning from you; I'm glad to know that you had a good experience with us as well. We had a fabulous class, and I must brag on Jennifer - she didn't let that bad interview experience get her down! She had another interview last week; it was a working interview, and she went in ready for anything. She was hired on the spot, and we cried and celebrated with her this past week. I had to share that with you because I am so pleased and proud of her determination. Will you please pass that on to your colleagues for me?*

*Thank you again for your support of our ladies and our mission; it is always a pleasure to work with you.*

There is power and value in work, and landing a job can be a life-changing experience. Work provides meaning, purpose, the opportunity to learn new skills, and economic independence and mobility.

A tremendous example of empowerment through work is Tyler Walker, a four-time Paralympian (2006, 2010, 2014, 2018). As Tyler transitioned from years of training and competition to the workforce, he worked with the Athlete Career and Education (ACE) program. Tyler Walker knows about grit.

Tyler was born without the use of his legs. He grew up in the shadow of Cannon Mountain in Franconia, New Hampshire, and started skiing at the age of six – quickly developing a passion for ski racing. He participated in local adaptive ski programs at Waterville Valley and Loon Mountain, and in 2003 at the age of 17, Tyler qualified for the US Paralympic Alpine ski team. He was a member of the team for 15 years, retiring after the 2018 season. While he was training and competing, Tyler earned a bachelor of arts dual degree in geography and international affairs from the University of New Hampshire.

Tyler's grit was tested in 2014. Leading up to the 2014 Sochi Olympics, he was in the best shape of his career. Mentally and physically, he was at the top of his game, and he had an excellent shot at medaling in Russia. Sochi was his third Paralympic Games, and with his experience and training, he could visualize himself on the awards podium. But during the downhill competition in Sochi, Tyler experienced a horrific crash. He lost control of his monoski and went airborne; his body violently bounced off the snow as he somersaulted down the mountain. He was airlifted off the slope via helicopter and taken to a hospital.

For the next four years, Tyler worked relentlessly, rebuilding his body physically and his spirit emotionally and changing his equipment in preparation for the 2018 Paralympic Winter Games in Pyeongchang, South Korea. Tyler says of those four years and the recovery process, "It takes your whole life, your whole being." At the 2018 Paralympic Winter Games in Pyeongchang, South Korea, Tyer won silver medals in the men's sitting slalom and men's sitting giant slalom. Over the course of four years, Tyler experienced the emotional extremes of being exceptionally prepared and then entirely broken, and finally in 2018, rising to excellence on the podium in Pyeongchang.

Courage. Endurance. Resilience. Grit. These soft skills are highly valued by employers, and Tyler has them in spades. What he lacks, however, are the hard skills. That's where the Adecco Group US Foundation was able to help and support him as he transitioned from his competitive life as a Paralympic athlete to a new chapter and career.

Through the Foundation, we funded a scholarship for Tyler to attend General Assembly in Denver, Colorado. General Assembly is a leading digital educator offering full-time and part-time courses in web development, data science and analysis, user experience design, digital marketing, and product management. After completing General Assembly's full-time immersive program as a software engineering student, Tyler will graduate with the hottest digital skills in demand in today's economy.

"When I finally decided to retire from ski racing," Taylor says, "I had done almost everything I could do with the sport. I'd had a lot of success and countless amazing experiences with great people. But I wasn't sure what I would do next."

Tyler knew he liked developing websites, but he didn't have enough hard skills to offer people. So he sought to remedy that.

"Through the support of Adecco, the USOPC ACE program, and the Adecco Group US Foundation," Taylor says, "I was offered an amazing opportunity to attend General Assembly's program. I am now more interested than ever to enter into a career in web development. The support from the Foundation has been instrumental in realizing this goal, and I hope they can help many other athletes after me to go down this career path."

Like the young man who threw the starfish back into the ocean, through small acts of kindness and generosity, we can all make a difference to one person at a time, and help to make the future work for everyone.

# Cherry on Top # 13: Live A Cherry on Top Life

I have two favorite personality traits that I admire in others. Previously, I talked about personal courage. The second personality trait I most admire in others is generosity. For me, generosity is an expression of love. When we have a selfless approach to relationships, we put the wants and needs of others before our own. Sharing our time, talent, and resources with others is a precious gift. The cherry on top is generosity – the selfless abundance mentality that puts others first. Always.

"Kindness is the language which the deaf can hear and the blind can see."
— Mark Twain

In your work and home life, develop Cherry on Top habits. Always ask yourself, "How can I make this better?" "What would take this event from ordinary to extraordinary?"

In 46 countries, the Adecco Group has a unique program, "CEO for One Month." In the United States, thousands of college students apply for one of 10 spots at CEO for One Month Bootcamp during which the finalists compete to earn this coveted title. Bootcamp week is exciting and intense for the participants, with every minute planned to give them the best possible experience, and for the judges to determine the most qualified candidate to represent the US in the global CEO for One Month program. The schedule is packed with a variety of events: sunrise workouts on the beach, team-building events with non-profit groups, an Italian cooking class, meetings with Adecco Group leadership, and high-pressure presentations. It's an intense but super fun week for everyone, and great care is taken to ensure that the finalists have an outstanding experience from start to finish.

In 2019, the announcement of the CEO for One Month was scheduled to take place on the oceanside patio of One Ocean Hotel in Atlantic Beach, Florida. The setting was beautiful, and everything had been planned "to a T," including the food and beverage, staging, decor, and press coverage. Two weeks prior to Bootcamp, I was reviewing the agenda and thinking about how to make it an even better experience for the 10 students. I asked myself, "What would be the cherry on top?" An idea popped into my head to have a plane fly a banner up and down the beach in front of the hotel announcing the CEO for One Month winner. We researched the idea and we found that the cost to have an aerial banner was within our budget and very easy to arrange and schedule. The banner did not take a lot of extra time, effort, or expense, but it was the cherry on top for the 10 CEO for One Month finalists, and it was definitely something they will remember about their Bootcamp week.

There are exhilarating Cherry on Top moments like banners in the sky and there are humbling moments that stay with you. When I was in high school, my father taught me a valuable lesson: things are not important. People are. During my senior year in high school, I was dating a boy named Phillip who I was crazy about. I was driving with him one day in my parents' car, and in my girlish high school way, I was trying to show off and impress him. That didn't work out so well for me or the car. At a stop sign, I wasn't paying attention, and I crashed the car, causing significant damage. Naturally, I was terrified to tell my parents about the accident and how I had wrecked the car by being careless. When I broke the news to my father, I was anxiously anticipating the lecture. Instead of being upset, Dad asked me if I was okay. I answered, "Yes, sir." He said, "Good, material things we can fix, people we can't." Dad was telling me that I was more important than a car – that what mattered most was me, and that I was not hurt or banged up in the accident. Dad truly has an abundance mentality and looks for the best in everyone and every situation, including wrecking the car. I treasure that memory.

When I was the senior vice president of the Southern Division, I started a tradition of opening our big annual kick-off meetings for branch managers with a surprise. One of my favorites was having an a capella group appear from the back of the room singing Heather Small's song, "Proud." In less than a minute, all 300 people were on their feet clapping to the beat and singing along. For another meeting, I invited the marching band from Johnson C. Smith University in Charlotte and they entered the large ballroom meeting space with their horns blazing and their drums pounding. The room was charged with super high energy and the meeting was off to a great start. However, the people having a meeting in the adjoining ballroom were not quite so thrilled and filed a complaint with the hotel conference manager. Lesson learned: If you have a marching band open your leadership meeting, make sure to first check with your next-door neighbors.

You don't always have to hire a band. Making small changes in our personal and professional behaviors can create impactful incremental gains. As Amy Cuddy told us at our meeting in 2016, "Tiny tweaks can lead to big changes." Think about the little things that you can do or the small changes that you can make in your life that will be a cherry on top for others.

It's easy to fall into a morning routine of arriving at the office, saying "Good morning," powering up the laptop, and jumping right into the workday with conference calls and meetings. The day flies by with us eating lunch at our desks, each person focused on their work and the tasks that lay ahead.

Sarah and I love our coffee in the morning, so we were delighted when Starbucks opened a new store in the lobby of our building. One Monday morning, we grabbed our coffee, returned to our office on the 14th floor, and sat down to share the stories of our weekends at the little round glass table that sat right outside my office. Ansley arrived shortly after and joined us at the table. This was the beginning of what we came to call "Coffee Talk." At the start of every day, we met at the little glass table to talk and review the plans for the day: what had to be accomplished, who was working on what, what was a priority for the day, and what was not. It helped us to stay focused on the "big rocks" and to be aligned on who owned what and the associated action items. Coffee Talk also became a time to share ideas, recipes, advice, stories, and generally to catch up on all aspects of our lives. We let the phone go to voicemail. Eventually, my direct reports understood that we had Coffee Talk every morning, and that I would return their calls ASAP.

Making a small change by scheduling 15 uninterrupted minutes every morning to talk and catch up has made a huge improvement in our communication and has kept us focused and on task the remainder of the day. If something comes up later in the day, we often say, "Let's talk about that tomorrow at Coffee Talk." Coffee Talk has become so much a part of our daily routine that we actually miss it when we are traveling or on vacation.

Scheduling personal time is paramount, as well. For me, the two very best weeks of the year are the annual family summer vacation we take at Sanibel Island the week of July 4, and Christmas week. I love these weeks for two reasons: they are super quiet work weeks when many people are "off the grid," and they are weeks spent with my family doing things that I love.

When I have time, I enjoy cooking and entertaining. Christmas Eve dinner at my home is one of my favorite occasions of the year. I start planning weeks in advance to make the evening and meal extra special for my family and guests. Someone once told me that I have "the gift of hospitality." Nowadays, very few people take the effort to set a table like I do – I spare no expense with the table setting. It brings me joy to spend the time to make sure that everything is perfect: the crystal and china are hand-washed, the silver is polished until my hands are sore, and everything twinkles and shines. When my guests arrive, the candles are lit, Christmas carols are playing in the background, the house carries the fragrance of our fresh-cut North Carolina Christmas tree, and the flower arrangements are "over the top" beautiful.

My traditional meal is Arroz con Pollo, a traditional Cuban dish (my maternal grandmother, Ruth Lillian Hodge, was born in Cuba). The side dishes include fiesta salad, Cuban bread, plantains, and the cherry on top is beef tenderloin served with my special horseradish sauce.

After a delicious dessert, we move to the game table. I try to be inclusive and play a game that a 3-year-old can play as well as a 90-year-old. One of my favorite games is Dog Bingo, and one of the highlights of the evening is our son Bryson serving as the Dog Bingo Caller: "The Whippet is a long, slender dog originating in England descended from the Greyhounds. The dog is Whippet." As Bryson is colorfully describing the dog in a very authentic British accent, the players are feverishly searching for a picture of a Whippet on their Dog Bingo cards. It's a lot of fun, but the cherry on top is the prize that goes to each winner of the games. Here's how it goes. As a winner, you get to choose between a wrapped box or a cash prize. There's lots of laughter and suspense as the choices are made and the boxes are unwrapped. In the box, there might be a Nespresso machine, a magnum of Dom Perignon champagne with six vintage champagne glasses, or a Jo Malone candle and Molton Brown gift set.

My hope is that when the evening wraps up at midnight, everyone feels as though it was the most magical Christmas Eve anyone could ever imagine. It's pure joy and happiness for me to host that evening.

I love giving gifts. It's important to me to take the time, thought, and care to pick out the perfect item for everyone on my list. It gives me joy to buy a gift for a family member, friend, or colleague that is totally unexpected and something that they would love (hopefully), but never splurge on for themselves. I shop all year for Christmas presents, and when I see something extra special, I buy it and put it away until December.

When I was planning Bryson's 6th birthday party, I considered all the usual themes: Superheroes, Beanie Babies, clowns, and others. But I wanted to do something special, something that would surprise and delight my 6-year-old son. When Hugo the Hornet, the mascot of the Charlotte Hornets, rang the front doorbell during his birthday party, Bryson was "off the charts" thrilled and ecstatic, as were Coleman and all of the other children. Hugo posed for pictures and signed autographs, and I believe that a few of the grown-ups asked for a picture with Hugo as well. Although Bryson enjoyed having his friends to his house, the cake, and his presents, Hugo the Hornet was definitely the cherry on top of Bryson's birthday party that year.

Living a Cherry on Top life means approaching every situation and interaction with joy and optimism, and taking care to be attentive to all the little things that comprise the whole. The cherry on top is not just one thing. It's the cumulative impact of being thoughtful, kind, and considerate, and having a spirit of helpfulness and generosity.

We get to choose how we live our lives, how we treat others, and ultimately, how we will be remembered. Don't miss the moment to go above and beyond to bring joy and happiness to others. Always put a cherry on top.

# Cherry on Top Lessons

- People are Your DNA

- Talent is the Biggest Rock in the Jar

- Culture Always Beats Strategy

- Service Never Goes Out of Style

- Business is Personal & Relationships Matter

- Retention of People Has a Direct Correlation to Profit

- Go to the Fire

- Your Boss is Your Best Customer

- Outwork the Competition

- Pay Attention to Detail

- Never Let Anyone or Anything Change Who You Are

- Make Your Last Job Your Best Job

- Live a Cherry on Top Life

Made in the USA
Middletown, DE
02 March 2020